TRUSTED TO THRIVE

How leaders create **connected** and **accountable** teams

MARIE-CLAIRE ROSS

Copyright © 2022 by Marie-Claire Ross

All rights reserved worldwide.

All Rights Reserved: No part of this publication may be replicated, shared, redistributed or given away in any form without the prior written consent of the author/publisher or the terms related herein. This ebook is licensed for your personal use. This ebook may not be resold or given to other people. Thanks for respecting the hard work of this author.

Limit of Liability: This publication is designed to provide accurate and authoritative information in regard to the subject matter covered. However, no guarantee of results is given. The use and outcome of tips and methods shared in this book are the responsibility of the reader.

ISBN: 978-0-9924196-5-3

Published by: Trustologie®, Melbourne, Australia
Visit the author's website: http://www.marie-claireross.com

Table of Contents

About the Author 1
Acknowledgements 3

Introduction 5

The Basics 11
   From Apathy to Achievement 13
   Trust – The Rocket Fuel to the Achievement Zone...................25
   Three Oppositional and Supporting Trust Forces.......................37
   How to Embed a System of Trust in your Teams 55
   The Roadmap – 9 Trust Building Strategies 71

Practice 1: Fostering Safety 73
   The Importance of Physically Safe Workplaces 76
   The Importance of Psychological Safety 78
   The Difference Between Trust and Psychological Safety 80
   Strategy 1: Reducing Interpersonal Risk 83
   Strategy 2: Showing Support..95
   Strategy 3. Fostering Learning 105
   Key Interaction: Meetings and One-on-Ones........................... 111

Practice 2: Creating Connection 127
The Challenges with Connection 130
Connecting the Pieces 131
Strategy 1: Linking Personal Impact 133
Strategy 2: Understanding Beneficiaries 143
Strategy 3: Focusing on People and Parts 165
Key Interaction: Visibility 187

Practice 3: Stepping into a Meaningful Future 195
Craving Certainty 198
Communicating to Create Certainty 200
Leveraging the Gap 201
Strategy 1: Understanding the Current State 205
Strategy 2: Identifying the Gap 221
Strategy 3: Working Towards a Future State 229
Key Interaction: Accountability 243

Wrapping Up and Next Steps 257

Further Resources 263

Connect with Me 265

Book List 269

About the Author

Marie-Claire Ross is a trust leadership speaker, facilitator and coach.

She started her career undertaking market research for some of Australia's biggest brands. Then, co-founded a video production house with her husband filming live television and creating safety induction videos. During her time leading Digicast Productions, she also wrote the book, Transform your Safety Communication.

Learning how to build businesses and lead staff became a quest. In the end, she realised video production wasn't her passion. In 2014, she took the leap and started the company, Trustologie®, which helps senior executives, leadership teams and middle managers build trust within their teams and improve performance. She works around the world in organisations such as QANTAS, Novartis, Petronas, Pitcher Partners, Australian Tax Office and Seasol International.

Marie-Claire lives with her family in Melbourne. When she is not training or writing, she can be found running, cooking vegan meals, renovating heritage homes or out in nature.

Acknowledgements

Many clients, mentors, friends, family members and staff have contributed over the years to help me not only understand the principles in *Trusted to Thrive*, but help me live them.

Thanks to some of my earliest supporters who helped me validate and fine-tune my approach - Alick Osbourne, Kristy Dam, Brett Lunn, Guy Mycroft, Harvey Martin and Jim Landau.

In addition, thanks also goes to those who I interviewed for this book or in the past - Damian Bridge, Mark Tannen, Simon Phillips, Michael Lambert, Ian Rourke, Jeff Rathgeber, Tina Robinson, Kate Morris, Gary Allen, Divan Gladwell, Andrew Murphy, Richard McCarthy and Grant Jackson.

I also wish to express enormous gratitude to my beta readers who gave me helpful feedback and advice - James Woodyatt, Tina Robinson and Lani Beer. Thanks also to Nikolay Hsu and Garry Undy who unwittingly tested out my new work and to Sam Sturgess for being the impetus for me to lead with trust.

And a big shout out to some of my mentors past and present - Col Fink, Matt Church, Lisa O'Neill, Angelique Rewers and Phil Dyer for their wisdom and guidance.

This book would not be what it is without the unique energy and insights of Kelly Irving - a master structural editor. As well as Lu

Sexton who edited the book and Lauren Butler who tirelessly proofed it.

Finally, a big embrace to my two daughters, Arielle and Amelie, who forced me to truly live *Trusted to Thrive*, as we endured an uncomfortable home environment during the pandemic while I wrote this book. Showing me that my model not only is important for workplaces, but families as well.

Introduction

In a hip, Melbourne hotel cafe, I am sitting in a dimly lit booth opposite Damian, CEO of a midsize company. Upbeat dance music is blaring and it is hard to hear the soft-spoken man who has made a career of turning around poor performing companies into star performers.

We are at the end of my interview about high performance teams and our coffees are all consumed. Taking a deep breath to collect his thoughts, his voice gets stronger as he reminisces, 'When I think of a high performance team, I think back to the most successful team I ever led. We grew the organisation from $110 million to $280 million, in just under three years. It was a really tough competitive environment and we didn't think we could do it. We would get together and brainstorm new strategies and then get to work executing them. I didn't lose one key person throughout those intense years. We had camaraderie where we all trusted one another to do the right thing. Everyone knew what everyone was doing and there was mutual respect and care for one another. We'd work long hours during the week and then we would even catch up socially on weekends. One of the managers died last week. The whole team was at the funeral, many of us flying in from all over the country. It has been years since we have worked together. Seeing everyone again, it was almost like we hadn't been apart. I miss being in that team and I want that in my current team. You can't beat it.'

Damian isn't the only leader to passionately tell me their experience of being on a team that kicked goals, despite the odds. Over the years, speaking on stage about high achievement teams, I often get pulled aside by leaders who want to tell me their experience. Their eyes are lit up, electric. Their luminance only fading when they quietly despair that they haven't been able to recreate that experience.

As humans, we want to be with other humans and be part of something bigger and better than we can create on our own.

> **We love being part of an energetic team that has plenty of solutions, excited discussions and productive activity.**

But the world has changed. The pandemic has separated teams, as it has separated friends and families. We no longer have the luxury of impromptu water cooler conversations, celebratory dinners or face-to-face brainstorming sessions.

Many people are in survival mode. Ground down by the relentless uncertainty, adherence to lockdown rules and the inability to be around people.

Leading a team effectively has been turned on its head. And it's unlikely that we will go back to how things used to be. Now, leaders need to know how to engage teams that are a mix of both remote and office-based employees.

This requires a shift in leadership style. One that fosters connection, when team members are disconnected by location.

And the question is, how do we create an organisation that enables employees to feel inspired, energised and innovative, when they are not connected face-to-face?

INTRODUCTION

It is a question I asked myself back in 2004, a couple of months before I had my first child. Back then, I worked in a video production company that I co-founded with my husband. We had staff in regional Victoria who helped us film and broadcast live greyhound racing. I knew that once our baby was born I was unlikely to regularly travel a six-hour return journey to catch up with them.

I had to work hard at building connection with my young employees, many of whom were from disadvantaged families. Back then, that meant monthly phone calls to check that they were all right – not just with the work, but in their personal life – and sending them inspirational books or food when things got tough in their world.

And what I learnt was that it doesn't matter where you or your team work. What matters most is the energy and focus you put into creating your team culture. And the most successful team leaders work on building a foundation of trust. You build connection through building trust. Trust is the beating heart of your team.

> **When you build trust as the team environment, you can put your team anywhere and under any conditions and they will thrive.**

A team that trusts one another, and their leader, creates magical team coherence. That wonderful space where you are all in flow, moving as one, reading each other's intent and body language. Like a group of professional dancers effortlessly moving in harmony, in tune to the rhythm of a song.

It creates a positive buzz, a hum, an energy that we crave. And it's a place where we thrive as human beings, where we feel energised and empowered, connected and aligned through shared identity and purpose. We feel valued, creative and safe to share our opinion. It's a place where we feel that all is possible, that we're in this together and that the hard work is worth it.

Despite the trials and tribulations, it's an unforgettable experience that we hold deep in our hearts for the rest of our life. Feeling trusted makes us proud of our achievements and motivates us to keep going when things get tough.

In her book *Powerful*, Patty McCord credits Reed Hastings, the CEO of Netflix, as saying, 'What people most want from work: to be able to come in and work with the right team of people – colleagues they trust and admire – and to focus like crazy on doing a great job together.'

The good news is that even when teams are dispersed, you can still create thriving teams were people feel at ease, and as a result are happier, healthier and more productive overall.

And that's what this book is about. How to create that wonderful, supportive environment where we feel trusted, and equally importantly, where our direct reports feel trusted.

> **As a team leader, you have the power to lead others into that beautiful place where we become better human beings.**

In this place we care and support one another, leaving our personal insecurities aside, in service of making the world a better place.

Over the last eight years, I have undertaken research inside companies and interviewed hundreds of CEOs and executives about how they build connection and trust with their employees. I've also interviewed hundreds of team leaders and employees about how they need leadership to build trust with them. I've read countless research papers and books on the topic. And I have coached leaders and facilitated training inside organisations, testing my theories and models to find out what works in today's workplaces.

What I have found is that building trust is all about a leader who has consistently practised the right combination of skills that fosters a thriving workplace environment. It's about a leader who has taken the time to understand and observe the human condition – what drives people to be their best and what shuts people down – and who compassionately responds to each individual in a manner that suits them best.

This is what this book will help you achieve: a deeper understanding of the human condition and what you can do to create an environment from which motivated people can flourish.

How to Use this Book

The backbone of this book is my *Integrated Trust Building System*, which I have developed and refined over the past eight years working with clients. You may be familiar with a similar model first proposed by Christine Comaford in her book *Smart Tribes*, and more recently popularised by Daniel Coyle in *The Culture Code*.

While their models have done an excellent job of explaining the factors our brains require to feel safe at work (safety, connection, future), my research within companies found that employees need specific interactions to build trust in dispersed workforces.

There is no right way to build trust, but this book describes the best way I know how. It draws on neuroscience, biology, psychology and sociology research.

My contribution is a synthesis of the best ideas clever leaders have uncovered, as well as what I have found works well in my leadership training and coaching practice. The strategies I cover will be relevant to anyone looking to create high performance with dispersed teams during change and uncertainty.

The book is broken down into four sections. The first section, The Basics, provides the context that you need to understand before we go deep into the *Integrated Trust Building System*. The remaining three sections all relate to the main components of the model. At the end of each section, there are activities and case studies to help embed the learning. You will find self-reflection questions, implementation ideas or a summary. You also have access to extra resources at the end of the book, which you can apply.

Thank you for picking up this book and being willing to take this journey. I look forward to being your guide.

Are you ready?

The Basics

Why Improving our Interactions
Makes a Big Difference

From Apathy to Achievement

Leading a high performance team is a bit like taking a team on an exhilarating elevator ride to the 150th floor of a building: encouraging your teammates that you are going to reach the top – fast.

Imagine a team where the leader encourages everyone to meet at the ground floor. The lift arrives and they all enthusiastically jump onboard. Even though the journey might be a bit scary, employees know they have the support of one other and their leader. People talk excitedly about where they are all going and what it will look like. The result is the team reaches goals almost effortlessly – riding express all the way to the top, without any stops or breakdowns.

In contrast, imagine a team where only 80% turn up on the ground floor to get onboard. People get in, but they avoid looking at each other and there isn't much talking. A couple of them are anxious, but instead of talking about it, they secretly push some of the floor buttons, so the team has to stop every other minute. Others join at different floors, missing out on important information or the opportunity to connect to others. No one takes responsibility for slowing the team down nor asks questions about where they are going and why. Everyone is too frightened about the future.

What's happening here is that interpersonal risk is at play. Interpersonal risk is a fear that people won't think highly of us or will reject us altogether. It stops people from sharing ideas, raising concerns or feeling connected to others. It impacts psychological safety, which is our ability to take risks and make mistakes, knowing that we will still be supported in our team.

In a highly popular TEDx video, Amy Edmondson, a Harvard Business School professor, talks through her research on the impact of accountability and psychological safety in teams. She discovered that when high levels of psychological safety and accountability collide it leads to high performance.

Ensuring people feel safe isn't enough to lift performance, nor is solely focusing on results; there needs to be a balance between the two.

A study by Zenger and Folkman analysed 400,000 360-degree survey results. They found that the most successful leaders possessed a powerful combination of competencies. Of leaders in the top quartile, 66% possessed both a focus on *results* and *interpersonal skills* (the ability to develop and maintain relationships). Meanwhile, only 13% of leaders who focused on *results alone* and only 9% of leaders who focused on *interpersonal skills alone* reached the 90% percentile.

> **Focusing on both results and interpersonal skills ensures there are fewer people issues to handle. In other words, there is less friction on the journey to the top.**

Both psychological safety and accountability are modelled and managed by the team leader. The way a leader models and rewards behaviour creates the culture in which a team operates.

To help leaders better understand psychological safety, I have created the Achievement Zone Model (Figure 1 overleaf). Amy

Edmondson's work has been the genesis for four zones of team performance, as well as some of the work I have done with teams over the years.

These four zones represent where we are currently performing and the impact that has on our teams. You might notice the zones also represent where team members are located and the overall performance of your team. Let's unpack these four zones in more detail.

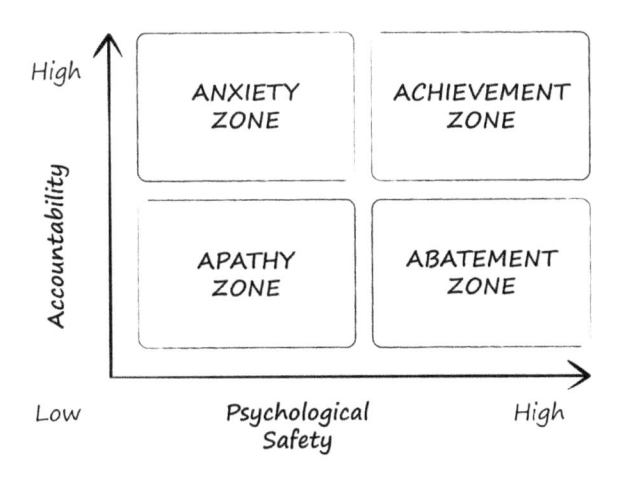

Figure 1: Achievement Zone Model

Apathy zone

When leaders create low psychological safety and low accountability, you will often find employees who are pretty disengaged. This can be one of the riskiest teams to work in, which results in employees not working too hard. Energy is spent on self-preservation – either because they are afraid of doing the wrong thing or they are exhausted and burnt out.

In this team, there's a lot of blame, cynicism, gossip and disdain towards leadership.

There are a couple of reasons for teams being in the apathy zone.

Sometimes it can often be the result of an authoritative, emotionally volatile leader who is closed off to their direct reports and who unwittingly creates a psychologically unsafe team culture, a leader who doesn't particularly enjoy leading people or prefers doing the technical work themselves.

Other times it can be the result of under-management. Under-management and micromanagement are on the opposite sides of the management spectrum. But they are both devastating to team and company performance.

Under-management occurs when a manager does not supervise their direct reports enough. It's when they avoid performance conversations, don't show up to meetings or ignore important issues. They rarely communicate or train people and are noticeably absent.

This can be due to a variety of reasons, such as having too many projects to juggle, feeling overwhelmed with work, or not having the right leadership competencies to supervise employees. Sometimes it could be that the leader feels uncomfortable calling out poor performance issues and doesn't want to be labelled a micromanager. They just want to be liked – by everyone.

Under-managed employees may appear to have more freedom and autonomy, but they feel ignored, unsupported and unsure as to whether their work is right or not. The onus is on the employee to manage client expectations, engage their manager and get them involved – a leader who they don't trust to be there for them.

What's interesting is that under-management is an expensive problem that most organisations don't really understand. And the difference is trust. Under-managed employees tend to under-perform because they are not guided on how to properly care for customers. It ends up that customers become frustrated and don't trust the company to do a good job. It shows up as a reduction in repeat sales and an upswing in customer complaints. It can even mean increased liability costs.

Apathy zone teams can also occur in an organisation that's had a poorly planned merger or where there has been some toxic behaviours played out at the top. This zone is incredibly low in trust and high in turnover.

But not only can our teams be in this zone, so can we. This is when you wake up in the morning dreading work. Not so much because of the work itself, but usually because you don't want to have to deal with customers or certain colleagues.

We can also fall into this zone when we are actively looking for another job or have found it.

Abatement zone

In this zone, leaders are often uncomfortable improving themselves and subsequently are uncomfortable pulling people up for poor performance. Or they are not being held accountable themselves. I come across a lot of teams in this zone that have had a big success in the past and are still coasting on their past achievements.

This comfortable and mind-numbingly boring place is when leaders create psychological safety, but don't hold their employees accountable for excellence. This is the confusing employee engagement result that points to high employee engagement in a team, despite poor productivity. In this environment, employees have no incentive to stretch themselves, be proactive or creative.

Performance here is abating. Employees believe they're doing a good job but have no desire to improve or even think differently. They feel comfortable in processes and rules, refusing to improve them, even when they are outdated and cumbersome.

As Joseph Grenny, a social scientist, discovered in his research, bosses are the source of accountability in mediocre teams. Team members will escalate problems to their boss to solve, only work nine-to-five and lack the motivation to move beyond their task list. It is a particularly difficult zone for high performers, who resent the lack of work ethic and the low competency levels of their peers.

Sometimes we feel that working in a comfort zone is a good place to be. But it's where ideas go to die, people coast, problems don't get solved and where groupthink reigns supreme.

Interestingly, trust across teams here is a big issue because other teams cannot rely on those in the abatement zone to meet deadlines and/or produce high quality work.

If you are taking the easy road in your work, you are in this zone. This could be because you still feel exhausted from a previous win, or perhaps you have personal or health issues that you are struggling with. The result is you take it easy because you don't have the energy to learn new things, work differently or encourage your people to be accountable. This can mean you get frustrated by directives to change and you justify the status quo. Sometimes you are in this zone if you have a boss that doesn't challenge you, so you start making excuses as to why you haven't met your goals.

Anxiety zone

Teams in this zone are high performing and can often be lauded throughout an organisation for their work ethic and focus on results.

But this is a psychologically damaging work environment as the focus is on outputs, rather than people.

I have found that there are two types of anxiety zones. The first one is where employees are worked hard, criticised profusely and have little support from their leader, teammates or other teams. Typically, it's a competitive environment where staff are pitted against each other due to the false belief that this will make them do better work. Employees often complain about 'feeling bashed up' when they present ideas at meetings.

There can also be a lot of micromanagement, which breaks trust with employees. Constant interference by a leader results in poor employee engagement, low productivity and high turnover.

It can even be when the organisation itself keeps a close watch on employee activities. Examples include using artificial intelligence to assess the work of employees working from home by tracking the amount of time spent clicking links and opening software. Other times, it's when individual results are rewarded rather than organisational outcomes. It's where busy work or time in seat is prized, rather than improving the system.

The second type of anxiety zone is where resources are stretched and the team has to do the bulk of work under difficult conditions in limited time. This has been prevalent for a lot of teams during the pandemic.

In either of these cases, stress, burnout and workplace injuries are major issues. Feelings of not being valued or appreciated also rise to the top.

This zone is common in demanding environments such as IT, legal, finance and medical. Interestingly, some purpose-driven organisations can often be found here because they reward behaviours that are aligned to the purpose. However, they often confuse rewarding achieving purposeful outcomes as being a success indicator, rather than the right behaviours to achieving them. Meaning that toxic behaviours can run rampant as they hide under the guise of purpose, therefore, masking the real impact to staff wellbeing.

I have even found teams in this zone who are in safe environments, but due to old legacy issues, have taken it upon themselves to work hard. Even when management has changed and they're working in a completely different environment, they still feel disconnected and unsafe.

The anxiety zone is often full of watermelons. This is when the progress of a project goes from red straight to green, instead of the regular red, amber then green. Typically, people are too fearful to report when a project is going amber because they're not going to make a deadline.

You really feel it when you're in this zone. This is when you feel quite anxious and under pressure to deliver. You're working long hours and don't feel valued. Sometimes you even feel misunderstood by leadership and wish they understood your workloads and challenges. Your mental health and wellbeing suffers, which can take a big toll on your family or personal life.

Achievement zone

This occurs when a team leader creates stretch goals, challenges direct reports to improve and strongly believes they can achieve. A lot of leaders approve small incremental improvements to goals. But a leader in this zone treats employees like athletes pushing them to continually improve – breaking their best records, not by a few degrees but through dramatic improvement.

Achievement zone leaders foster a supportive environment where employees learn and work together, focus on continuous improvement and explore exciting new possibilities. After all, people don't tend to spontaneously stretch themselves, but need the support of a leader who fosters the right environment to grow and learn. In this environment, people are not only encouraged but also thrive on the autonomy to work how they want and contribute to high level decisions.

An achievement team is all about attunement – shared goals, shared risk, shared work, people helping each other out and collaborating at a high level.

This zone is where things start to shift and you reach a powerful tipping point in performance. Efficiency improves dramatically and your team is regularly kicking goals.

Candour is also high in this zone. You can talk about performance issues and people embrace feedback. It's where people are learning, adapting and open to change. This is where you can introduce a new strategy that you've developed with your team and people will work as long as it takes, without complaining, to get it done because they know they have the support of everyone around them.

The achievement zone team only occurs when the leader leads by example, works hard to ensure they are trusted by the team and encourages team members to trust one another. For hybrid teams, this has become critical.

You know when you're in this zone when you feel excited about going to work in the morning. You look forward to solving problems with others and making progress. You love to learn, share new insights and envision an engaging future. It's when work feels like play and you are so engrossed in your work that you lose track of time. In fact, you would even turn up to work for free because it is so enjoyable.

Life here is really amazing, almost spiritual – reverential, even. This is where we trust the world. It's where we feel so connected to the vision that we know we're making the world a better place. This is the zone where happy memories are made. It's a time that we look back fondly on for years to come.

Unfortunately, we don't stay at this level for long. It's unstable. Forces outside of our control can slam us without any warning, our team members can freak out and create unnecessary drama. And we can often drop out of this zone when there are too many unknowns rocking our world.

Not only that, for driven leaders, if we are here for too long, we get bored. And the tendency here is to meddle and cause chaos. That's because in this zone you don't get the immediate feedback loops of improving things like you do in the other team zones. This requires leaders to regularly reinvent their leadership and take on side projects that can re-energise their enthusiasm.

The truth is that how we get to this zone, and remain here, is through trust. It all comes down to the leader creating a collaborative, thriving environment that lowers people's innate fear of being rejected by the team. It's where we trust our leaders, our team members and ourselves.

If you don't feel that you have your team in the achievement zone, or you want to know how to stay there for longer, this book will show you what to do.

Reflection

- Where are you right now? What could you achieve if you could move yourself up into the next zone? How would it feel to more easily access the achievement zone?

- Where is your team? If you could get your team from apathy/abatement/anxiety to achievement, what impact would that have on your overall productivity? What about your happiness levels?

- Where are your team members right now? If you think about the median person on your team and the way they are engaging, what would moving them into a higher zone have on teamwork? And what about your job satisfaction levels?

Trust – The Rocket Fuel to the Achievement Zone

There is a time in every manager's or leader's career when they ask themselves: *How do I get others to trust my leadership? And how can I trust others to get work done?*

Trust is at the cornerstone of all relationships. We sense its presence in healthy relationships and its absence when relationships turn sour.

When employees trust management and the organisation, they are more likely to exchange ideas and information, discuss difficult issues and find ways to create synergy.

But if people don't trust, they close down. It means they won't contribute in meetings, collaborate or try anything new for fear of retribution. They react negatively to one another, working in stealth to get things done in order to access resources and budget. They create chaos, rework, recriminations and workarounds.

Trust is essential. Without it, social groups can't function properly.

Without trust, there is no meaningful connection between people. It's just meaningless coordination.

It is trust that shifts a group of people into the achievement zone. It provides people with the security to explore the world around them. Inspiring people to commit to actions, make decisions fast and confidently buy into a big vision. It helps reduce unnecessary friction so that things get done with ease and speed.

Otherwise, it's like working in sludge. People block one another, require countless meetings to reach consensus and hoard information and resources.

You might be thinking that trust seems like a fuzzy buzzword, but it lies at the heart of every business issue.

> **What starts as a people problem,**
> **becomes a productivity problem,**
> **which becomes a profit problem.**

Trust might be a small word, but it is a big, complicated topic. Part of the problem is that trust also means different things to different people.

When it comes to improving trust, it is really important to understand in concrete terms what it means first. Having clear language around trust gets everyone on the same page. A definition that I use for workplace trust is:

> **The ability for everyone in an organisation**
> **to confidently rely on (and predict)**
> **that others will do the right thing and**
> **make good on their promises.**

After all, in a workplace, reliability is key for teams to work seamlessly together when there are different priorities, challenges and goals. Trust provides the safe environment for people to thrive during change and uncertainty. It is when people think the best of people and situations, rather than assuming the worst and defaulting to believing others are mistreating them.

There is no doubt that trust is an important capability for leaders to master. Ask any leader whether trust-building is important and they will agree. The problem isn't *knowing that trust is important*; it's *knowing how to frequently and consistently build trust*. And more importantly, it's about making it a daily part of how you interact with others, even when you're tired, reeling from a negative event or dealing with people you don't like.

In the work and research I undertake within organisations, I have found that leaders often have misconceptions about leading or how they build trust with others, which reduces their ability to influence. The three main misunderstandings with building trust are:

1. Technical skills are seen as more important than relationship-building
2. Trust is one-way
3. Trust is assumed

Let's look at each of these in detail.

1. Technical skills are seen as more important than relationship-building

The workplace of today is fast moving, complex and features dense interdependencies. The days of being able to accurately forecast the future and estimate what will happen is no longer relevant. Things can change in an instant.

Twenty-first century work is no longer about how many widgets staff produce, but how well they make them together.

In our interconnected world, businesses thrive through idea generation, partnering and innovation from teams of highly skilled experts. Yet, this isn't easy when most teams are dispersed and striving to manage changing client expectations, tight resourcing and multiple stakeholders.

The reality is technical expertise is no longer enough to stay ahead of the curve. The seeds of success are communication, co-operation and adaptability. This requires leaders who know how to build trust among team members and with different stakeholders in dynamic conditions.

Unfortunately, most leaders feel that they need to keep updating their technical skills. This is partly because our school and tertiary education systems reward us with competing against others and being the best. Then, workplace training predominantly focuses on technical proficiency rather than soft skills. This is further compounded by business environments that motivate employees to compete against each other for promotions, sales targets and budgets, which encourages leaders to act opportunistically, hurting their careers and the organisation long term.

The world of work today requires a new leadership style. Leaders who have the right combination of technical, interpersonal (the ability to develop and maintain relationships and enlist others) and intrapersonal skills (self-management and self-awareness), as shown in Figure 2.

TRUST – THE ROCKET FUEL TO THE ACHIEVEMENT ZONE

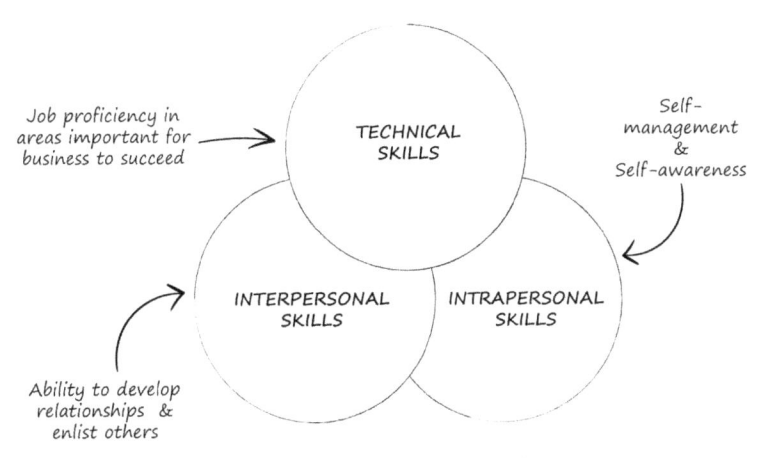

Figure 2: Employee skills for today

Instinctually, we focus on our technical competencies. The skills we can see in action. Often, leaders focus on their technical abilities, not realising that it's their people skills that matter most when they become a leader. Unwittingly, they break trust with others when they fall into micromanaging and perfectionist tendencies. Preferring to do the work themselves than to trust others with it. But they're missing the point of being a leader.

The role of a team leader is complex, requiring a mix of both management and leadership skills. Management is about setting, measuring and achieving goals, training employees, building systems and process, budgeting and dealing with daily work. Leadership is about connecting people to the bigger picture and the meaning behind work, guiding others and alignment around goals. Both are important and require balancing technical, interpersonal and interpersonal skills.

> ***Counterintuitively, individual expertise doesn't matter as you progress in your career. What matters is how we interact with others.***

Don't get me wrong: technical skills are important. But as your career advances, the real leadership difference is interpersonal and intrapersonal skills. These are the skills of leaders who get the best out of their people and, just as importantly, who manage the different priorities and goals of various stakeholders instead of pushing their own agenda.

2. Trust is one-way

We are biologically programmed to look out at the world and determine whether we can trust those around us. But we aren't designed to look at ourselves to see whether we are behaving in a trustworthy manner.

Any business relationship is a social contract between one or more people. Yet, we often don't realise that trust is measured in both directions. While we're sizing other people up as to how trustworthy they are, they're also assessing whether we can be trusted. Thanks to our biological wiring we spend more time protecting ourselves from others than actually considering what signals we're sending out about our own trustworthiness.

Despite what other trust gurus might tell you, trust is not about getting others to do what you want. Yes, it will help you on that journey, but real trust building is about co-creating a solution that benefits everyone. Not just yourself.

Usually leaders will tell me that they want to build trust so that their team will do work right, other teams will collaborate better with their team, and executives will trust what they are doing. While this is all important, what few realise is that trust is reciprocal. It requires honest self-awareness to assess where you are not being trustworthy. Are you turning up to work on time? Are you owning and fixing up your mistakes the best of your ability? Do you truly understand what the other person wants so you can deliver to their expectations?

When we don't take the time to understand each other's expectations, the relationship becomes unbalanced resulting in each side questioning the other's intent.

The following table reflects the three areas I commonly see where leaders want to be trusted but fail to fully appreciate other stakeholder's expectations.

Inwards – how team leaders want others to build trust with them	**Outwards** – how others want team leaders to build trust with them
1. I want to trust my people to get work done right and on time.	**Top leaders:** Want to trust that you are doing the right things to challenge employees in their role, do great work and uphold brand reputation. **Direct reports:** Want to trust that you support their career goals; will do the right thing by them when they make a mistake; judge their performance on outcomes achieved, not time in seat; trust that they are working when you can't see them. **Your peers:** Want to trust that your team will deliver on time and on standard.

2. I want trust between the frontline and leadership (not always so readily considered).	**Top leaders:** Want to trust that you are communicating their strategy in an energetic and understandable manner to help them with changing culture. **Direct manager:** Wants to trust that you will make their job easier. **Direct reports:** Want to trust that executives care about them and have their best interests at heart, before they back a new initiative or change. **Your peers:** Want to trust that you are motivating and aligning your team to the same vision.
3. I want to trust leaders in other teams to do the right thing by me and my team.	**Top leaders:** Want you to provide a holistic understanding of the interactions between all the moving parts across an organisation, in order to reduce silos. **Direct reports:** Want to trust that other teams can be relied upon and are enjoyable to work with. **Your peers:** Want to trust that you are sharing information, resources and insights with them to improve their performance, not just your own.

As a leader, it is a complex job to manage a variety of stakeholder expectations. This can only be done when you take the time to understand their needs and perspectives. And deliver to that, rather than to what you want.

3. Trust is assumed

A lot of leaders make the mistake of assuming that they have trust – either because of their position, personality or past efforts.

Trust takes time and effort to build. According to a Watson Wyatt 2003 study, it takes seven months to build trust and half that time to lose it.

One of the mistakes leaders commonly make is that they assume that to build trust you have to treat everyone the same. But it's not true. You have to build trust with each person differently and frequently.

Trust is like a battery. If you leave a fully charged battery alone, charge slowly disappears. If you aren't proactively building trust, it is declining. Never assume people trust you. Increasing your team's trust is a process, not a single event.

It requires being intentional and understanding how to build sustainable, long lasting relationships with everyone around you, not just with those who are strategically important.

This is a big task because each person around you varies in their propensity to trust based on their tolerance to risk, personality characteristics, life experiences and level of power.

What Holds You Back from Successfully Building Trust?

Every leader knows that trust is important. The problem is that being good at fostering trust, with everyone, is hard.

What I have found is that most leaders do little to increase trust, not because they don't want to, but because they aren't sure where to start. Many managers will spin their wheels attempting to fix it or waste time and headspace focusing on the wrong trust drivers.

The underlining cause is that no one is taught how to build trust or to act in a trustworthy manner in the workplace. Worse still, some receive training by those who operate from the perspective that trust is a currency that can be wielded to get what you want. While that might have been true in the past, it is not anymore. Such a narcissistic perspective is quickly losing traction.

Because leaders don't understand trust comprehensively, they focus on improving a couple of behaviours they value, such as being consistent or telling the truth. But this wastes time and effort if these behaviours are non-consequential to specific employees. And these behaviours are not easy to get right all the time. For example, sometimes we don't know we're acting inconsistently and we can't discuss confidential information, so we can't always tell the truth.

We live in a diverse and complex world. Some people might need you to spend more time understanding their needs or explaining the context, while others are good to go. But it's not as simple as just understanding people better.

Unfortunately, there are also a lot of things working against us to reach the high trust achievement zone. I call these the Three Oppositional and Supporting Trust Forces, which we'll delve into next.

Reflection

- What do you focus on – improving your technical or interpersonal skills? Where are you most comfortable?

- How do you think about what other people need from you – to trust you?

- Do you assume people trust you? What do you do to ensure you are regularly building trust with people?

Three Oppositional and Supporting Trust Forces

Have you ever started a new job or worked with a new team and realised that you needed to build trust quickly?

For many leaders, managing trust in teams is a challenge because there are three different forces at play. It's important to understand these main dynamics so that we can mitigate the damage they can potentially cause when mismanaged. To save time and reduce frustration, you need to know what you can control and what you can't.

As you can see in Figure 3, the three forces are:

- micro trust forces, which are within ourselves,
- meso trust forces, which are between team members,
- macro trust forces, which reside outside of the team.

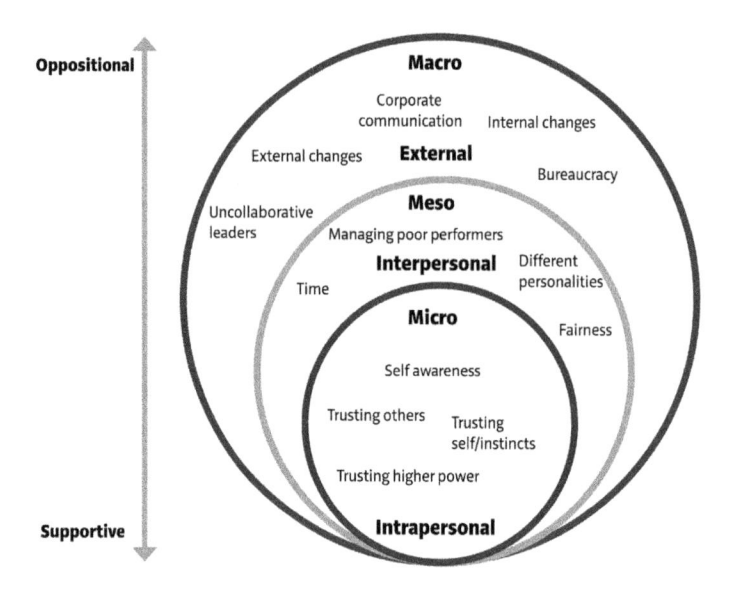

Figure 3: Three oppositional and supporting trust forces

We send these forces out to people and they send them to us, so they are multidirectional you could say and impact us in six different ways.

Force 1: Micro trust forces

Micro trust forces are critical to our ability to lead. These are our intrapersonal skills – our ability to self-manage, adapt to changing circumstances and learn new things. Micro trust is underpinned by self-awareness and understanding that the only person we can change is ourselves. We can change how we react, interact and behave, as well as what we believe. At its core, it's about how much we trust ourselves.

> **Trusting ourselves is foundational to our ability to lead. It impacts how we lead our teams, the performance of our direct reports, how other leaders view us and how we cope with change and pressure.**

This is the only force we have any real control over. However many of us aren't aware of our behaviours and mindsets that are sabotaging our efforts to step into the achievement zone. The fact is if we want any sort of change in our team, we have to change our own behaviours. Changing from the inside-out magically transforms how people react and interact around us. This requires understanding behaviours that no longer serve us and modifying how we think and approach things.

When I talk to high trust leaders who have built successful careers and been phenomenal at leading people, they have one key thing in common: they trusted themselves. They felt that people needed their guidance and that they were equipped to give it. They believed in themselves and their people.

Of course, there is a fine line to be drawn between those who authentically believe in themselves and those whose belief stems from a shallow, ego-driven perspective that is blind to how others feel. The best leaders are confident in themselves, but they always include others and embrace different perspectives. They know they are not always right, unlike a narcissistic leader whose leadership is all about fulfilling their needs and excluding others.

Let's take a look at the different types of micro trust forces that are impacting us daily.

Self-awareness

Dr Tasha Eurich, in her book *Insight* discovered that self-aware people have two types of knowledge: internal and external self-awareness. Internal self-awareness is knowing who you are, what makes you tick and your patterns of behaviour over time, while external self-awareness is about understanding how other people see you.

In general, human beings aren't very self-aware. But we think we are. Eurich found that even though most people believe they are self-aware, only 10 to 15% of the leaders she studied actually fit the criteria.

As mentioned previously, we are biologically programmed to look out into the world to see if we can trust what's going on. But we aren't designed to look at ourselves to see whether we are behaving in a trustworthy manner. This is why an unaware leader has no idea how their behaviours are creating distrust.

Often, I coach well-meaning leaders who receive poor trust results from their direct reports and peers. They feel hurt and betrayed by their 360-degree ratings, failing to understand how their behaviours have led to such a result. These leaders tend to be low in not only internal self-awareness, but also in external. Over time, I help them understand how their behaviours are unintentionally creating trust issues.

Interestingly, before I work with them, they tend to rate themselves 10 out 10 for their ability to build trust with others. After attending my workshops or receiving mentoring they rate themselves lower – six or seven.

You might be wondering: *How can a leader rate themselves lower for trust when they're working on improving trust?* I have to say when I first experienced this, I was devastated that my work wasn't getting the right results. But what I learnt was that it's a healthy sign. They are becoming more self-aware and slowly getting rid of old beliefs and self-protective biases.

Over the years, I've worked with hundreds of leaders and what I've found is that external ratings are the only valid method to assess how trusted you are at work – *not* your own personal opinion.

THREE OPPOSITIONAL AND SUPPORTING TRUST FORCES

Leaders who rate themselves highly for trust are typically not rated that highly by their peers and direct reports. Trusted leaders realise that building trust is an ongoing journey and that they need to build trust every day. This takes self-reflection and honesty as they truly look at how they are managing themselves, their time, and other people.

While low trust results can be devastating for many a poorly performing leader, the truth is there is no better method to bust through blind spots than receiving reality-based information of how people see us. No matter how hard it is to accept.

In a high performing and supportive environment, good leaders actually see these results as helping their career, not damaging it. Research by Carter Cast in the book, *The Right (and Wrong) Stuff: How Brilliant Careers are Made and Unmade*, indicates that job proficiency simply isn't enough. Without self-awareness and the ability to work well with others, managers' and leaders' careers are at dire risk of derailing.

Typically, leaders that lack self-awareness are more likely to be performing in the anxiety, abatement and apathy zones, blissfully unaware of how their performance is impacting others and their job security. They tend to be blindsided by other leaders opposing them, due to poor work quality and lack of timeliness.

> *If you think you're great at building trust, you probably aren't.*

The good news is that creating a high trust achievement zone will naturally encourage team members to be more self-aware. Continuous improvement, embracing feedback and encouraging personal agency all work towards employees understanding themselves better.

Trusting yourself

> *'A bird sitting on a tree is never afraid of the branch breaking, because her trust is not on the branch but on its own wings. Always believe in yourself.'*
>
> Charlie Wardle, *Understanding & Building Confidence*

The most important person we can trust is ourselves. When we make a mistake, receive harsh criticism or miss a goal, it can be too easy to lose trust and confidence in ourselves. This is detrimental to our leadership capability as our decision-making abilities falter when we fear making the wrong choice.

When we don't trust ourselves to lead or we don't think we are worthy of being a leader, other people feel that and automatically don't trust us. They feel something is wrong with the energy we project. While they might feel our power or capabilities, they will be confused as to why we don't own them.

Being a successful leader means learning to trust yourself first and overcome the highly common imposter syndrome. Interestingly, you can tell if your colleagues don't trust themselves when they make bogus excuses about why they can't do a particular task. They will also go behind your back and make complaints about you, rather than tell you directly that they cannot do a particular job. This can be confused with people not feeling safe enough to share the truth, but sometimes it is more about their ego being in defensive, self-protection mode.

The key to being trusted is to be trusting.

Don't let an inability to trust yourself make you an arsehole. Most of the toxic behaviours we see in workplaces are displayed by people who are afraid of admitting they don't know what to do or who doubt their own abilities.

The fastest way to move forward as a leader is to accept where you are and envision how you wish to lead. It requires being persistent, taking ownership of your weaknesses and having faith that you have a right to be in charge.

Leaders who don't trust themselves tend to not trust others and the situation. At a deeper level, how you trust others is a reflection of your own fears and insecurities. If you don't trust yourself, it means you operate from fear rather than from a positive and expansive outlook. You are subconsciously working to protect yourself, rather than working for the interests of your people or organisation.

Trusting your own instincts

Trusting ourselves means trusting the little voice in our head that warns us when we need to spend more time building trust with those around us or improve our job competency.

Andrew Murphy is an engineering director from Melbourne, Australia. During the height of the pandemic, he decided that being a self-employed trainer was no longer feasible because face-to-face workshops were no longer an option. He accepted a new job in a software company, but it didn't last long.

Reflecting on why his job didn't work out, Andrew felt disappointed with himself that he ignored and questioned his own instinct. He said, 'I felt like a lot of the time my instinct would tell me something and I'd disregard it. After my first online meeting with the UK CEO, as soon as I left that meeting, I knew I needed to check in fortnightly with him. I didn't do it. And I feel that little things like that contributed to not building enough trust.'

All was not lost. Andrew learnt from that experience. He accepted a new engineering director role in a midsize company reporting directly to the CEO. Within the first two weeks, he booked one-on-ones with all the heads of departments and everyone in his team. Not only that, he organised monthly catch-ups that were put into everyone's calendars.

Focusing on building interpersonal trust at the start of a new job, built trust remarkably quickly in lockdown. He shared, 'My personal belief is that there is no shortcut to building trust. But there are ways to speed it up and get there quicker. Instead of taking a year, you can reduce it to a month or two. In my new job, I spend a lot of time building trust with my counterpart in the US. We have a weekly one-hour long one-on-one. Most of that time is social, the rest of the twenty minutes is work. But when I read an email from him, I can hear his voice. There are fewer misinterpretations. That was the biggest change. In my previous job, I didn't get the trust of my UK CEO and he didn't believe I was acting in his best interests. Now, my peers and my direct reports know I'm working with the best intentions. We can still disagree and have a more productive conflict as opposed to them worrying whether I'm trying to undermine them. Trust speeds up and smooths out the conversations that arise through having a job.'

Your ability to trust your inner voice is critical to modifying your behaviours resulting in stronger relationships. It also ensures that you listen to your own counsel, rather than default to others whose advice might not be appropriate. Leaders who fail to listen to their 'inner ding', often miss out on important opportunities to improve their effectiveness.

THREE OPPOSITIONAL AND SUPPORTING TRUST FORCES

Trusting a higher power

Sometimes change and uncertainty are so intense and uncomfortable that you have to ride it out.

Developing your inner ability to trust is crucial. At some level, it requires trusting that everything is going to work out, that you are being looked after by a benevolent force, even if you can't imagine how that will possibly happen at that point in time.

In his book *The Power of Habit*, Charles Duhigg reported on some research within Alcoholics Anonymous that correlated the effectiveness of spiritual beliefs and staying sober. The data indicated that alcoholics successfully stayed sober until a stressful event impacted their lives. At that point, no matter how many good habits they had built to abstain from drinking, it wasn't enough to stop them getting back on the wagon.

In contrast, alcoholics who believed in a higher power were able to make it through tough periods still sober. Believing in God didn't matter, it was the belief in a higher power or in something bigger than ourselves. Or at the very least the belief that things will get better.

Sometimes this means surrendering to a situation and allowing things to change, pulling back from fighting oppositional forces or ceasing to support others (who give nothing back).

Force 2: Meso trust forces

Next are the trust issues that occur more within the team domain that you have some control over, but still need to navigate to get right.

At the meso level, trust is impacted by what team members think about one another and their leader. These can be supportive or oppositional, depending on the personalities in your team.

To some extent, external or macro forces also play a part. This requires a team leader that has strong interpersonal skills. In other words, they have the ability to build strong relationships because when it's needed, they know how to approach conflict, communicate change or provide negative feedback. Learning how to improve in these areas is important to developing trust in your team, with your direct reports, your peers and leadership.

Let's go into these in more detail.

Taking the time to build trust

In today's fast-paced business world, you often don't have the luxury of time to decide whether someone is trustworthy or build trust with individual team members, direct reports, colleagues or other unit leaders. Teams must be put together quickly, decisions made and deadlines met.

Even when you do have time, you can get so caught up in your own deadlines that you miss out on important opportunities to connect with others and cultivate trust leadership. Or you take shortcuts – preferring to use email for important conversations.

Relationships take time to build. Nurturing high trust relationships involves investing the time to understand direct reports and the priorities of peers. It requires really listening to people about their concerns, needs, priorities, goals and acknowledging what's on their mind. However, the good news is that the effort is worth it. When we don't take the time to connect fully with people, we risk damaging trust. Strong leaders realise that when they have trust with their people it means they spend less time checking up on them, worrying about a project, or sorting out issues.

THREE OPPOSITIONAL AND SUPPORTING TRUST FORCES

Managing poor performance and perceived fairness

One of the most common mistakes a manager can make is that they don't want to pull people up for poor performance because they don't want to hurt people. They feel that if they do, it will cause issues in the relationship, making things difficult, that they will become distrusted and not seem 'nice'.

While this feeling might appear to come from a good place, more often than not it's really because managers prefer to do what feels good to them, as opposed to doing the right thing by others.

The reality is if there is one thing I see time and time again, it's managers who are distrusted by their direct reports because they don't tell people the truth, they avoid providing their direct reports (or peers) with honest feedback. They don't realise that most people actually prefer to know if they've made a mistake.

This is a big one and it's common across all industries and business sizes.

> *If there is one thing that causes distrust in a team, it's when a poor performing employee is allowed to continue working, even though their performance is dragging everyone down around them.*

This also includes toxic behaviours and actions. Often, the team leader becomes the source of distrust because they haven't done anything to remove the offender. Not only that, it gives license to others to perform or behave below standard. This is a common issue in the abatement team zone.

Then, there is always the difficult balance between allowing people privileges such as being able to leave early, which can sometimes reduce perceived fairness levels in a team. Again, this is another area where a team leader can receive complaints if other employees don't receive the same rewards. It creates distrust and a lack of confidence in leadership because it reeks of a failure to confront issues and a protection of the status quo.

Knowing how to improve performance through coaching or managing favouritism takes maturity and experience. It also takes courage. But if you want to be promoted to senior leadership positions it is fundamental.

As difficult as it is for many leaders to have candid performance conversations, trust in their team will always remain below par until performance and inequity have been acknowledged and dealt with.

Managing different personalities

Any workplace brings together people who would have little to do with each other outside of work. Having the skills to unite a variety of people into a cohesive team takes time.

It starts with team leaders willing to spend the time to understand each individual. This involves regular conversations to learn each team member's communication and work styles, and clearly specifying how they, the leader, likes to receive communication and prefers to work.

Furthermore, it requires making the time to connect other team members in team meetings, not only to understand each other but also to connect what work each team member undertakes and how their work adds value to the team.

Force 3: Macro trust forces

Macro trust forces are either external to the organisation or part of the internal fabric of how work is done overall in an organisation's architecture. From my work with leaders, I have found that leaders contend with macro forces on a regular basis.

These can be the most frustrating and anxiety provoking as they are outside your locus of control. They come in a variety of forms.

External volatility and internal changes

Savvy leaders understand that their team members crave certainty and look to them for reassurance, so they work hard at being honest, open and supportive. Yet, there are so many things beyond a leader's control because things can change quickly. There is external volatility ranging from erratic weather patterns to pandemics, marketplace changes to game-changing technologies, international trade terms to government restrictions.

Then, there are internal organisational changes, including new CEOs, restructures, mergers and acquisitions, new team members and product shifts.

Communicating honestly about what is going on in an organisation isn't always possible, or legal. Some leaders struggle to manage the tension between being transparent and predicting the future with meeting their leadership obligations.

Bureaucracy

Employees trust a workplace on three levels: the organisation, leadership and their peers. Executives are responsible for ensuring that employees can see and feel evidence that the organisation itself can be trusted to do the right thing.

Organisational trust is determined by a combination of its rules, policies, systems, values, strategies and behaviours, and how these are designed, enforced, communicated and rewarded by leadership.

Employees trust their organisation when systems are designed to protect all stakeholders fairly and with minimal red tape.

> ***Trust thrives when employees see evidence of consistent action and behaviour that indicates good intent.***

Realistically, the relationship employees have with the organisation itself is impersonal. After all, companies aren't living beings. The relationship requires leaders to step in and be the bridge to interpret the policies and procedures and help employees understand how their job role is serving the greater good. Unfortunately, this is where many well-meaning leaders become frustrated with corporate bureaucracy that appears to unintentionally work against them.

The larger an organisation becomes the more policies and procedures. These are designed to protect the organisation, but they can also slow it down. HR, financial, procurement and legal decisions are often cumbersome, disjointed and lack day-to-day strategic reality.

Furthermore, corporate communication fails to resonate with employees who have an uncanny ability to reject any messaging where the intention behind its creation is questionable.

> ***Policy-based communication that is written to protect the company (or certain individuals) creates resistance from employees who want to see evidence that the company understands and cares about them.***

It becomes a challenge for leaders who are tasked with inspiring their team to commit to the company vision when corporate information demonstrates a lack of caring for people.

As one director from an engineering company said, 'I spend 10% of my time on admin and 15% buffering my team from the organisation so they can do their job. They're aware I do that because they hear from other teams about how difficult things are. I get accolades because they know I filter and buffer and make work more enjoyable.'

Strong levels of trust drive strong performance and more consistent success. When employees have a high level of trust in management and the organisation, the company as a whole becomes significantly better at achieving business goals and undertaking change.

Reflection

- Which force would you say is impacting you the most right now?

Putting the Three Trust Forces into Practice

Leading a team isn't easy. You can often feel like you are caught in the middle, between doing the right thing by leadership and your employees. All three trust forces come into full swing – both oppositional and supportive.

Take Anne, one of those rare leaders who is often put in charge of teams because she can transition teams from wallowing in apathy to thriving in achievement. In a previous role, Anne led a team of 22 direct reports across New South Wales and Canberra.

As she says, 'When there are too many changes that have not been managed well, people stop trusting leadership. That's when I was called into this role to manage a poorly performing team. I am the sort of person if someone needs to be performance managed I'd be called in, because I would respectfully have the conversations and give clear communication about what was expected. When expectations weren't met, then I'd have another conversation, asking in a compassionate manner, "Is this the right place for you to be?" I hate having those conversations, but I was one of the very few people in the leadership team who would have them.'

So while she was diligent in managing trust at the meso or interpersonal level in her team, it was the macro level trust forces that became trickier to manage. She added, 'I felt like I was the person caught in the middle trying to manage this team with all these challenges, but then still trying to be respectful of a leadership team I was not starting to trust. I realised I was burning out and the executive team weren't showing me respect anymore. Everyone below me was fantastic, but trying to support the top was not working because they were not being honest.'

THREE OPPOSITIONAL AND SUPPORTING TRUST FORCES

> In the turmoil, Anne began to doubt herself and resigned. This is when she spent more time at the micro level – reviewing her behaviours and better understanding her leadership capabilities. She reflects, 'I questioned whether I could lead a team and whether I'm a good leader. The last five months has been a journey on some of those micro things. Looking back, I probably too blindly trusted people. My instincts told me "this is not okay, I shouldn't be treated this way, my wellbeing is not being cared for." I've done a lot of reflection and had faith in God that things would change and be different. And I'm about to start leading a new team in a company with a better culture. I am a hopeful person and I'm self-aware, so there were a lot of things I learnt during the process that reminded me that I am resilient. I do trust people and my instincts were right. I have been reminded that those are things you need to hold onto. I also know that I did leave a really great legacy of leadership when I left and I have great skills for this new role.'

How to Embed a System of Trust in your Teams

Thousands of years ago, when humans roamed the African savannah, it was in our best interests to live in tribes. Being part of a tribe allowed us to sleep soundly knowing that others were looking out for sabre-toothed tigers.

We are biologically programmed to want to be with people and work together, as we instinctively know it helps our survival. Yet, there is a dark underside to this need to be with others – we also fear rejection. In fact, neuroscience studies have uncovered that we experience social rejection like physical pain.

We are constantly evaluating our level of interpersonal risk in our teams and workplaces. This subconscious fear drives us to weigh up whether or not to make a comment or stay silent.

Our brains scan our environment four-to-five times a second to make sure we are safe. While we no longer have to fear tigers, in the workplace, we are subconsciously cautious about our teammates.

When we first start working with a company or a new team, we quickly assess whether the team leader and our teammates can be trusted. We carefully conserve an image that we are competent. We avoid asking silly questions, speaking up about our concerns, sharing information or reporting errors. In other words, we avoid the critical elements for team discussions that we need to have to improve performance and avert disaster. As it happens, these are also the very factors we need to feel fulfilled in our jobs to perform optimally.

This is where the importance of leaders kicks in. I believe that one of the most important capabilities for a team leader is to create a thriving, safe team environment that decreases interpersonal risk.

As Amy Edmondson explains in her book *The Fearless Organization*, the free exchange of ideas, concerns or questions is routinely hindered by interpersonal fear more often than most managers realise.

After all, it's this interpersonal fear that inadvertently pushes people into bringing their worst selves to the workplace. When you have a team leader who is abusive, teams will be dysfunctional. Conflict and fear rule. Contrast that to a team with an empowering leader and you will find a team talking openly about issues and fixing them. Collaboration and transparency reign.

Whether your team members display low trust or high trust behaviours all comes down to you – the team leader. Interestingly, a lot of leaders put up with low trust behaviours believing that is how people are – that their personalities are fixed.

> **But the truth is, as a trusted leader, your leadership abilities encourage people to engage in productive dialogue rather than avoid it, to strive for achievement, rather than wallow in a comfort zone.**

HOW TO EMBED A SYSTEM OF TRUST IN YOUR TEAMS

Your goal is to move people from the low trust behaviours below into the corresponding high trust behaviours:

Low trust Team Behaviours	High trust Team Behaviours
Avoid productive dialogue Evade confrontation. Act passive aggressively. Conflict with others. Churn on issues after meetings.	**Engage in productive dialogue** Progress issues leaving minimal relational scars. Discuss faults to improve.
Stay in comfort zone Set comfortable goals and minimal accountability. Afraid of change.	**Strive for high performance** Hold each other accountable. Push for ambitious goals. Future focused.
Focused on individual function Lack of interest in others, competitive, not supportive.	**Focused on team** Interested in others, extend support. Take up difficult tasks.
Silo thinking and operating Protect turf and resources. Prioritise own goals.	**Foster transparency** Collaborate and share resources and information for the greater good.
Stale meetings Individual reporting with little decision-making, constructive debate or idea exchange.	**Dynamic meetings** People listen to one another, report errors, challenge the status quo and make fast decisions. Finish energised and focused.

A common misperception by leaders is that trust will come naturally to their team.

The reality is that you can't bring a talented group of people together and expect them to gel and work seamlessly. It is up to you to tirelessly reduce interpersonal risk for each individual and within the team.

In fact, the top team at Google learnt this the hard way. They would hire the most accomplished employees and throw them all together, expecting that would create a high performance team. To their dismay, this recipe didn't create a good team, let alone a high performance one. So they decided to investigate.

Four years and millions of dollars later, Google fastidiously conducted over 200 interviews with Google employees across 180 active teams to study the validity of an astonishing 250 attributes that affect teams. Attributes such as, were the best teams made up of people with similar interests, people who were motivated by the same rewards or people who socialised outside work hours? In the research study dubbed *Project Aristotle*, they even sifted through half a century of academic studies on teams. Google researchers reviewed team after team. The results were astounding. None of these commonly valued attributes was important. What Google discovered was that who is on the team doesn't actually matter. What was critical was how the team functioned together.

> **It doesn't matter who is on the team.**
> **What matters is how they interact.**

And it all starts with leaders; leaders who model the right trusted behaviours fostering the best environment for their team to thrive.

As a leader, your main task is to foster a warm environment where interpersonal risk is low and trust is high. It's about taking the right actions to build trust, rather than just paying lip service to it, because you both model and drive your team's social dynamics and performance.

Of course, not everyone will follow you. Each person has their own path to follow in life. Some people will choose the higher ground, others feel more comfortable blaming others and playing the victim. It's their choice. All you can do is be exemplary in your behaviours and gently coax people to join you. Not everyone will. In fact, expect to face some challenging criticism from those who just aren't ready to play nicely. But you can be reassured that if you provide the right conditions and some people aren't thriving, then you know that they are not a right fit. It makes it easier to let people go because you can clearly see how they are behaving in ways that are detrimental to achieving client outcomes.

Now, you might be thinking how are you going to create the right environment when you're already dealing with lots of priorities, complicated individuals or even a toxic culture?

The solution is an easy-to-follow system that automatically helps you build trust, so that building trust becomes a daily habit and a natural part of how you interact with others. This process helps rewrite the programs that we are born with and supersedes workplace interactions that no longer works for us.

In the pages that follow, I will share three main principles for building trust in your teams and with your peers. But first we need to take a peek inside our brain.

How the brain works

There are two parts to our brain: old and new.

If you think of the brain as an onion with lots of different layers, then the top layer, the one closet to the scalp is the newest one. This brain is the neocortex and it's the largest part of our brain. And it's the prefrontal cortex, the part at the front, that is important for executive functioning. It's where we make rational decisions, plan and innovate. When you laugh at a joke or find a solution to a customer problem, it's this part of the brain that's working. It's where the most complicated thinking occurs.

Down in the centre of our brain lies our limbic brain that has been with us since our days roaming the African savannah. The old part is not a thinking brain, but a survival brain. It's more primitive. It was primarily designed to keep us safe from danger. Allowing us to switch into fight, fright or flee mode.

It stores our habits and routines, so we don't have to consciously think about how to walk every time we get up in the morning.

In fact, our limbic brain processes over 400 billion bits of information per second but we're only aware of 2,000 bits (which really is mind-boggling, except for the brain of course!).

This essential brain hack help us do other important things, such as check how many followers we received on Instagram overnight or how to seamlessly match our shoes to an outfit.

Our limbic brain is responsible for our feelings, such as trust and loyalty, decision-making and handling stress. But the real kicker is that it has no capacity to understand language. That's why it's so difficult for us to put our feelings into words, particularly about a decision we've made or why we trust someone.

It's also why you can't tell people to trust you. A lot of people fall into the trap of thinking that they can fix trust issues by just telling people they need to trust more. Leaders will tell their team 'you can trust me on this' or my favourite, 'everyone tells me that I am trustworthy, you can trust me, too' If you have been on the planet for more than decade, those statements might make you feel queasy. And for good reason.

HOW TO EMBED A SYSTEM OF TRUST IN YOUR TEAMS

We process whether we can trust someone through our emotions. We don't trust others by what they say, it's how they make us *feel*. It's their consistent actions that show that they care about our wellbeing that determine whether we feel we can or cannot trust them. And that's why it's so common for employees to complain about their leaders not walking the talk.

> ***You can't talk your way into trust;***
> ***you have to behave your way into it.***

When we are stuck in our old brain operating system, we are in an unresourceful state of mind. It is a pretty limited and fearful perspective of what's possible for us. We work on the wrong tasks, solve non-existent problems or get stuck and don't know what to do.

Ideally, we are primarily operating from our prefrontal cortex. This enables us to see the big vision and work out the steps to get there. It's where we feel we have choice and can make decisions based on a more positive and expansive outlook.

To help us stay there, we need leaders who act more like *cheer*leaders: enthusiastic and vocal supporters who believe in their teammates, ensure they have the right resources and empower them to fulfil the company purpose. These positive leaders are enjoyable to work with and foster a thriving, accountable environment.

So how do leaders move people from survival and fear into a more resourceful and creative state? How can you assist people to work with their brains rather than against them?

You have to communicate to people in the right way that taps into their emotions.

The importance of emotionally resonant communication

As American psychologist Abraham Maslow taught in his hierarchy of needs, we can't concern ourselves with higher goals (self-mastery and purpose) until we have the necessities of life. Those being physiological needs (food and water), physical safety and social connection.

In a workplace, employees need confirmation that they are safe from harm and that their fellow workers are looking out for them. They need to feel connected and valued for their contribution.

At the same time, employees need to believe the work they do matters, that they are making an impact and there is a clear future for them within the organisation. That is why a company purpose is so important. If done well, it clearly specifies *how* and *why* the company makes a positive impact to the world and shows that the company has a fundamental reason for existence beyond just making money. This is important to counteract the natural suspicion and cynicism within our society that business is all about making a profit. Employees and customers trust organisations when they can see evidence that the organisation cares.

The reason a company purpose is so powerful is because it's the *why* – the emotional connection the business has to the world. Humans are emotional beings and they buy into their workplace based on how much the purpose resonates with their own values.

When we trust that the organisation and leaders will do the right thing by us, we can move up into the higher levels of contribution and creation. Our work provides us with self-fulfilment. We seek personal growth and stretch ourselves. In the right environment, we transition to the peak experience of being self-actualised. Maslow described this level as the desire to accomplish everything that one can; Mihaly Csikszentmihalyi, in his seminal book *Flow*, referred to this as the state of losing track of time because the work we are doing is so enjoyable.

If people are waiting for reassurances that they are safe and accepted by their team, they are more likely to focus their energies on survival rather than creation. They are unable to commit and believe in the vision. They wallow in victim mode, blaming others and avoiding responsibility.

Humans need to feel certain in their surroundings. After all, the old fear that they might be thrown out of the tribe and attacked by a tiger is still deeply embedded in their programming.

Trust gives us a sense of safety to explore and understand our world. It helps us reach the flow state and work at our highest level.

The Integrated Trust Building System

Neuroscience research confirms that there are certain factors that the brain requires to trust a situation.

Daniel Coyle asserts in his book *The Culture Code* that our brain asks subconsciously: 'Are we connected? Do we share a future? Are we safe?' Safety, connection and future are important for our brain to trust. In her book *Smart Tribes,* Christine Comaford found that employees require safety, belonging and mattering to trust.

In my work and research with clients, I have tweaked both those approaches and developed the *Integrated Trust Building System* (Figure 5). It lays out the steps and strategies to help leaders more easily create a thriving team environment for a range of different individuals.

This system also answers the questions people subconsciously ask themselves: *Is it safe to be myself? Do I belong here? What's my future with these people? Can I trust these people to look out for me?*

When these questions are answered affirmatively, it provides employees with the comfort they need to contribute and create rather than withdraw and self-protect.

If people don't subconsciously receive these assurances from their team leader (or each other), they hold back opinions, information and working with others. Behaviours their limbic brain feels will keep them safe. They stay invisible, procrastinate and feel unworthy.

Workplaces require leaders who reassure people that their emotional needs are being met through both verbal and nonverbal communication. Non-verbal communication includes using body language, eye contact, facial expressions and gestures, signals that help us interpret the real meaning and intent behind what someone is saying.

And with people working from home, this has become critical because it's easy to miss non-verbal signals that we notice when we are face to face. It is vital that leaders know how to communicate both verbally and non-verbally to the part of the brain that manages trust – the limbic brain. The part of the brain that doesn't understand language, but feelings.

This is critical to engage people emotionally and pull them into the achievement zone.

HOW TO EMBED A SYSTEM OF TRUST IN YOUR TEAMS

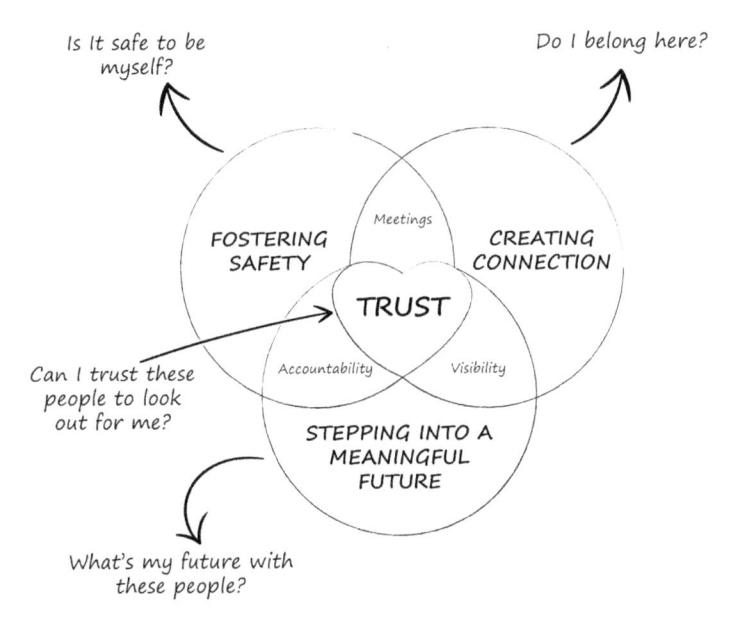

Figure 4: The *Integrated Trust Building System*

The *Integrated Trust Building System* helps leaders to focus on the three most important practices to emotionally engage employees, so that the limbic brain trusts the situation.

These are:

1. Fostering safety

This includes psychological safety that people can take risks or make mistakes and without it becoming 'a career-limiting' move. It also includes physical safety that people are safe from dangerous work and bullies, which can negatively impact their mental health.

2. Creating connection

When people feel like they don't belong, it creates self-doubt and fear. People need to feel a sense of connection with the group to increase their ability to succeed in their role.

3. Stepping into a meaningful future

When people don't know what's going to happen next and the situation feels unsafe, they will push back from committing to goals. The way to avoid this is to involve people in a meaningful future through clearly articulating the company vision and people's career pathway. This pulls people into engagement and out of the low performance zone in the brain.

> **These three critical practices catalyse to form trust, the beating heart of your team, which enables people to operate at a more sophisticated level.**

Think of these practices as being like ropes that help your employees feel connected to you. It's a bit like the tethers that keep astronauts tied to the spaceship so they don't float away in space. In space, astronauts leave the safety of the spaceship to do a spacewalk in order to carry out an experiment or test out new equipment. Every leader is like a spacecraft that supports their direct reports to explore, learn new things and work at their highest level. They provide people with the security they need to feel connected and protected to their leader and crew.

These three practices are interrelated. Sometimes improving safety can also improve connection. While talking about the future can improve both safety and connection, it's a mistake to believe these practices exist in isolation. Often, organisations focus on just learning about psychological safety, but this needs to also be combined with connection and future for maximum impact.

The trick here is to always touch on all three factors in your dealings with others, understanding the subtle nuances within each. Our brains are designed to need lots of signalling. You can do this not just through verbal communication, but also through subtle and consistent cues that help people feel that they are safe, connected and have a future. Interacting with each team member this way subtly tells people 'we're all in this together'. This helps people breathe more easily knowing they are supported and valued - making it much easier to face difficult challenges.

As Alex Pentland found in his research *The New Science of Building Great Teams*, how we communicate is actually more important to business success than what we communicate.

What many leaders get wrong is they believe being a leader means having the answer to every question, giving orders or a really long pep talk in a team meeting - in other words, through what they *say*. Yet, this can unintentionally send cues of non-belonging. When a leader ignores what people said, talks over them or angrily dismisses their perspective it signals that people aren't safe. Being trusted is actually about how you make people *feel* through what you *do* or even *don't do* that will build their trust in your leadership.

Working the System

The three trust practices (safety, connection, meaningful future) are what you need to regularly communicate to those around you to help them perform at their optimal level. Then, there are three corresponding interactions – meetings, visibility and accountability – where you practise emotionally resonant communication techniques.

These are the critical times when people are judging your behaviours to evaluate whether they can trust you. Each of these three interactions provide important opportunities for two-way feedback, ensuring that you are able to finesse what people need from you and what you need from them.

1. Effective meetings and one-on-ones

Employees are quick to complain when communication is unclear, when they are the last ones to know what's going on and when messages are inconsistent. When people complain about communication issues, it's because they suspect they are not being told the truth or not being told enough, or because the communication lacks clarity.

> **Humans need certainty. Communication is all about reducing ambiguity and creating clarity.**

Trust is enabled through communication. Communicating regularly openly and clearly to your people is an important action to build trust sustainably. Regular team meetings and dedicated time with your direct reports encourages transparent and honest two-way dialogue.

2. Fostering visibility

Visibility is key to building trust. People believe what they can see. They need to observe that they are in a safe place where there are no secrets, that their boss is supportive, that people aren't going behind their backs and that leadership cares about employees.

Visibility is a key tenet of transparency and includes visibility of information, priorities and progress both within and across teams, and in leadership behaviours. It is also an important capability of employees to visibly demonstrate they are working when they're at home or at the workplace.

3. Managing accountability

In a workplace, trust is inextricably linked to performance and capabilities. A high trust organisation switches on accountability, performance and people taking full ownership.

Accountability is two-way. It's about demanding accountability and being accountable. This means leaders act responsibly and take ownership for results – both good and bad – and demand that their direct reports do the same.

The Roadmap – 9 Trust Building Strategies

To help you understand all the pieces of the puzzle, I want to take you through a map that represents the key areas you need to focus on.

As you can see in Figure 5, each line represents three practices that form the structure of this book, together with three strategies for each practice to help you achieve them, totalling nine trust building strategies.

Key Practices				Key Interactions
Fostering Safety	Reduce Interpersonal Risk	Show Support	Foster Learning	Meetings
Creating Connection	Link Personal Impact	Understand Beneficiaries	Focus on People & Parts	Visibility
Meaningful Future	Understand Current State	Identify the Gap	Work Towards a Future State	Accountability

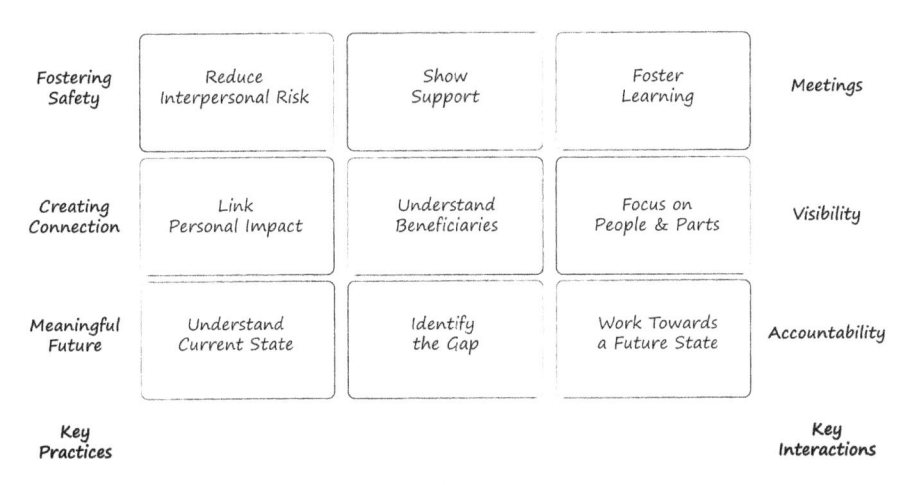

Figure 5: Integrated Trust Building Road Map

Practice 1 – fostering safety – explores how leaders can create both a psychologically and physically safe workplace environment through reducing interpersonal risk, increasing support and fostering a learning environment. The main interaction for this is meetings and one-on-ones.

Practice 2 – creating connection – breaks down how to communicate the meaning of work to people and conveying how their work helps others. This needs to be articulated through the broader context of how all the moving parts work within an organisation. The main interaction for this is visibility.

Practice 3 – stepping into a meaningful future – discusses how leaders can reduce uncertainty through being honest about the present state, pointing out any gaps in systems or capabilities to then be able to paint a picture of a wonderful future. The key interaction here is accountability.

The good news is that these three practices don't take much time to deliver, it just takes practise and courage. And when you get them right, they provide a powerful shortcut to navigating the complexity of human behaviours and beliefs. You can be assured that if someone isn't working out, it's more likely that they are not a right fit; they do not have the characteristics or behaviours to lift their performance in an environment that is supportive and rewarding.

Working on these three practices through their nine correlating trust building strategies ensures that you create a wonderful environment where your team can work well together in all sorts of situations.

Let's get started.

Practice 1: Fostering Safety

How to ensure employees feel safe,
in order to improve performance

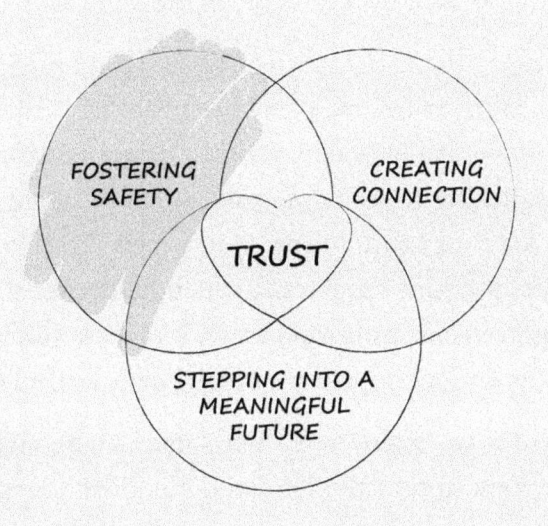

FOSTERING SAFETY

CREATING CONNECTION

TRUST

STEPPING INTO A MEANINGFUL FUTURE

A couple of years ago, my fourteen-year-old daughter had a restless night's sleep due to being awoken a couple of times from a cat meowing loudly in our backyard.

We lived in a street full of townhouses situated close together with garages out the back that all lined up, neatly forming a pathway for cats (and possums) to safely check out was going on in neighbouring backyards as they scurried along the gutters. Except this cat was different. He was not interested in having a sticky beak; he was frantically jumping into each backyard, meowing a lot, as if calling out for assistance.

Two days later, my husband and I went for an early evening stroll and were accompanied by a skinny, fluffy ginger cat. He was so eager to be with us, talking to us as we walked. He followed us home and seemed very keen to come inside. Concerned that his owners were on holiday, we gave him some food, which he devoured instantly. He spent the night on our front door mat, meowing softly to us as we checked on him by looking out the small window of the front door.

The next day we discovered from some neighbours that he was a stray, so we took him to the local vet. He didn't seem to belong to anyone. He had no microchip nor had he been desexed. As per the protocol, he was sent to the Lost Dog's Home (who ironically look after cats). Fast forward two weeks, we adopted him and brought him home. We named him Riley as the natural companion name to our other cat, Buffy (in homage to my favourite television series, Buffy the Vampire Slayer).

PRACTICE 1: FOSTERING SAFETY

Riley spent a week in our bathroom as we slowly introduced him to Buffy. Every time we would visit him, he would purr and be incredibly affectionate and happy. He initially seemed like such a people cat.

When we finally were able to let him explore our house, we discovered he was toilet trained and he knew how to use a cat flap (unlike our other cat who we had never been taught to use the cat door).

And once he settled in, we also found he didn't actually like being patted much at all. He would comically contort his body to avoid touch like a stretchy slinky toy. If we picked him up and carried him for longer than a minute, he would practically dive bomb out of our arms like an overly determined kamikaze parachutist. Yet, every night he would demand a long cuddle with our youngest daughter, deeply peering into her eyes with utter devotion.

It was estimated that he was 15 months old when we found him. We have no idea how he was treated by his former owners, but it's fair to believe that they were sometimes nice to him and sometimes not so much. He's never been particularly comfortable around men he doesn't know.

One thing for sure is that he doesn't want to be a street cat. He wants human company. He wants to be loved, valued and acknowledged just like a human. He loves it when I look into his eyes and tell him how much I love him. He also likes to meow a lot – letting us know if it's started raining, he's found a possum, and well, a whole lot of random stuff we're not sure about. But to also check that we are still there for him. He also loves the comfort of a warm bed and regular food. He never runs off and he is always around us. Yet, initially, he found it hard to be with us.

It took two years for Riley to feel safe in our home and to trust that we weren't going to abandon him like his previous owners. He's now the loving, affectionate cat we first glimpsed. Hanging out with us all day and night, not just with our daughter.

Riley is no different to how people are at work. We want a job that means being around people for the physiological benefits – money to pay for food, shelter and life necessities. We want to be physically safe, where we know we are not in danger of getting hurt. And we want the psychological safety that we can speak up, be heard and not get punished. We want the connection of people and to know that we are valued. And that our colleagues, our boss and the company care about us, that they are invested in building a relationship with us long-term. Many of us need to see a lot of positive actions and hear the right things to know and *feel* that we are safe at work.

When we don't get the right signals, it can bring out our dark side. We become inconsistent with how we act around people – feeling comfortable with some but avoiding others. Some of us might lash out, assume the worst, steal from our employer or colleagues and blame others for our own problems. While others stay small, invisible and keep their thoughts to ourselves. Neither is good for the workplace.

The Importance of Physically Safe Workplaces

Trusting others is a key component of being human. The relationships we have that make us feel safe are really important to us. And safety is on two levels: psychological and physical.

The COVID-19 pandemic really shone a spotlight on the importance of health, safety and wellbeing, elevating the relevance of health and safety messages as being so much greater than just 'health and safety on the shop floor'. Employees realised the value of the safety department's role in mental health and wellbeing of employees, both at home and at work.

PRACTICE 1: FOSTERING SAFETY

Since COVID, internal communication has become even more valued by employees as it demonstrates how much an organisation cares about their employees, providing comfort during uncomfortable times. Employees want heart-felt, engaging emotional communication that helps them understand why they should care about health and wellbeing.

Communication also highlights whether their leaders and the company itself can be trusted. Employees look up to senior leaders to see that safety is a priority and that they are safe from harm. Heartfelt safety communication bridges the gap between leadership and employees to demonstrate how much the organisation cares about people.

Our brain feels good when people care about us. We function better.

A Towers Watson Global Workforce Study of 32,000 employees from 29 countries found that caring was the most important thing leaders can do to create a high trust culture. Those who work with caring leaders are 67% more engaged than colleagues whose supervisors do not care about them. Respondents said that caring was more important than training, benefits or salary. It even increased employee retention.

Physical safety is judged as being taken seriously by an organisation when people have the right resources to work and live safely. Communication that promotes 'everybody must care about everybody' is disseminated and acted on and leaders avoid sending conflicting messages that getting things done more quickly is more important than safety.

To feel physically safe, people need to feel that their colleagues are also looking out for them. Employees can get so busy doing their work that they often don't realise that safety is about ensuring that they're not putting their colleagues into risky situations, unintentionally shoving people into the anxiety zone.

When companies care for their people, people thrive. Work gets done in communities and caring communities make work seem like play.

> **A lot of people confuse safety as being about compliance, but at its core it's about compassion for human life that sends the deeply emotionally resonant message that people are valued.**

In my previous work helping organisations create large safety training programs, I would turn up to the factory floor to direct employees as they were filmed undertaking processes. It was always enjoyable because people were so excited to be involved. They could see that the company was spending money on them to produce high quality training materials. You could almost visibly see the morale boost in employees during the training video production. It is no different to how many employees appreciated regular and critical communication during the pandemic.

The Importance of Psychological Safety

In addition to being physically safe, we need to feel that dealing with other people is not going to hurt us emotionally. For example, we need to feel we are not at risk of being bullied or that we will suffer from anxiety due to workplace pressures or toxic colleagues.

Psychological safety is different to physical safety because it's not so obvious when someone has been hurt. After all, if your boss makes a derogatory remark, you don't instantly get a bruise on your face. Instead, if you're in a really toxic environment, over a period of time you will get a range of symptoms from headaches, insomnia, stomach aches and strange body pains. Depending on your constitution these can turn into more sinister issues. A 2015 study by Eric Anicich from the University of Southern California, found a psychologically unsafe workplace increases our mortality rate. But it's not so easy to look at a workplace and see if it's psychologically unsafe. It remains hidden because most people outside of the team aren't aware of what is occurring. A lot of leadership behaviours that create a lack of psychological safety can be covert. To the CEO, the leader looks like a results-driven star, but to her team members she's a micromanaging control freak. The team feel unsafe, but complaints to HR about the leader's behaviour are ignored, so team members continue tiptoeing around their emotionally volatile boss and it becomes a tacitly accepted work routine.

To many direct report's horror, toxic bosses regularly get promoted for getting the job done at the expense of their team's mental health - irrevocably sending the wrong messages to employees that people don't matter.

If you've ever been on the receiving end of working with a dysfunctional leader, you know how devastating it can be to your wellbeing. It slowly chips away at your self-confidence and job fulfilment. And it can take years to get your mojo back.

But it's not just leaders high on the narcissism spectrum or with personality disorders that cause toxic workplaces. If we are under pressure, undergoing personal or health issues, we can often say or do things that make other people anxious without our awareness. We can inadvertently send employees into the part of their brain that produces a suboptimal performance.

The Difference Between Trust and Psychological Safety

Before we go any further, I need to point out a common confusion that psychological safety and trust are the same.

As Amy Edmondson says in her book *The Fearless Organization*, psychological safety is experienced at the group level. People tend to all agree on whether their team environment is safe. It's temporary and immediate. By contrast, they won't all agree on whether they can trust their team. That's because trust refers to the interactions between individuals. What it is or whether it is present differs for each person. Its existence is in the minds of each individual. It depends on the context, whether people can be relied upon and the organisation itself can be relied upon.

As I mentioned previously, trust describes an expectation about whether we can confidently rely on others and predict that they will deliver on future promises, whereas psychological safety involves our expectations about the immediate interpersonal consequences of a workplace interaction.

An example is Ben filling out a permit to work for a task. His boss tells him not to fill it out because the documentation will slow down the job and a customer deliverable. Ben does what he is told, putting his own physical safety and that of his co-workers, at risk. In other words, he trusts his boss is doing the right thing for the customer. He's prepared to work unsafely rather than face the immediate consequences from his boss for filling out the form.

As Edmondson says, 'Trust is about giving others the benefit of the doubt, while psychological safety relates to whether others will give you the benefit of the doubt when you've made a mistake or ask for help.'

In a workplace, we need to feel psychologically safe before we can trust a colleague or leader to do the right thing by us.

With that in mind, let's delve into the three main strategies for improving psychological safety:

- reducing interpersonal risk,
- showing support,
- fostering learning.

Strategy 1: Reducing Interpersonal Risk

We are constantly evaluating our level of interpersonal risk in our teams and workplaces. During our dealings with others, we subconsciously weigh up whether to speak or stay silent, help others out or not, rectify an issue or not, take on a difficult task or not. We choose looking good over being good, defaulting to what will impress our peers rather than doing the right thing by customers.

This can be debilitating for organisational life. People act like fakes. They end up being overly polite and deny that there are any issues. They are too fearful to say how they really feel, in case they lose status with their colleagues. The result is people gossip and blame behind people's backs, fail to reach consensus in meetings, disagree with data and slow down decision-making.

People who don't feel psychologically safe put themselves first. They don't trust other people will do the right thing, so they do what's right for themselves. These behaviours can end up being part of the culture, covertly damaging an organisation's future.

One definition of corporate culture is that it's what behaviours get tolerated. When leaders fail to confront harassment or withhold information, these behaviours flourish.

You can tell a team is low in psychological safety because their meetings are boring. Everyone is playing safe because they don't feel it. No-one wants to have a peek under the hood and see how performance can be improved. Self-protection, denial and staying in one's comfort zone rule.

Many leaders will tell me that their teams are great because everyone on their team 'gets along fine'. On the surface it may look like 'getting along' is a strength of a team. People share work progress and tasks. They may even engage in friendly chit-chat and make jokes. But cordiality can often hide passive-aggressive behaviours that avoid the tough conversations and constructive conflict. Occasionally, this might show itself as slight off-the-cuff comments.

What I often find is that people are secretly fuming and hurting from past transgressions. They leave the meeting and ruminate for hours about what occurred, then let off steam by complaining about what transpired with their bestie in the team.

People aren't talking about the mistakes they made or when they don't agree with the CEO's strategy. They aren't even really working together to do the right thing by the customer, because they're too busy doing the right thing for themselves.

Over time, innovation drops off, speed to market and business paces slows down. In these circumstances, you'll often find leaders retreating to the safety of their own function or business units to do the real work.

In an achievement zone team, people don't act in the typical ways that are intrinsically associated with job competency. They ask curious questions of each other and themselves, they laugh about their mistakes, apologise when they slip up and speak up about their concerns. Underlining these behaviours is the desire to improve – both themselves and others in the team.

STRATEGY 1: REDUCING INTERPERSONAL RISK

Think about your team dynamics:

- How openly are people sharing errors, in order to fix them?
- How often do team members challenge one another to think differently about what they're doing?
- Do team members like to learn together and solve problems?

One of your most important roles in leading a team is to ensure that everyone feels safe to speak up about issues, so you can fix things before they become much bigger problems. It's not easy because some people don't even realise how fearful they are of flagging issues.

It is vital for leaders to create a secure environment where people feel safe to be themselves and bring their authentic, whole selves to the table with their wisdom and know-how, as well as the humility to admit when they don't know something. This helps a group of people work together to debate and solve issues, rather than focussing on self-interest and false consensus. The outcome is true collaboration and faster decision-making.

Part of creating a psychologically safe workplace is to allow people to bring their whole selves to work. Delineating between work and personal life doesn't work; they are interconnected. Our work life impacts our personal life; our personal life impacts our work life.

Your aim in reducing interpersonal risk is to develop relationships with your team members so that you both are comfortable to talk honestly to each other about performance and behaviour issues, and how to fix them. It's about being more conscious and mindful of building relationships that encourage one another to grow.

To do this effectively you need to:

1. Focus on the achievement of collective results

2. Encourage speaking up
3. Change how team members discuss and receive issues

Let's look at each of these.

Focus on the achievement of collective results

"Individual commitment to a group effort: that is what makes a team work, a company work, a society work, a civilisation work."

Vince Lombardi, celebrated American football coach.

In low trust environments, leaders pit employees against each other under the false belief that competitive pressures will lift performance. Unfortunately, all this does is create an environment where people are out for themselves – hoarding information and not supporting others. It increases interpersonal risk and amplifies destructive behaviours.

In contrast, trusted leaders share and manage risk throughout a team. They focus on long-term impact, rather than short-term business performance. Instead of individual sales quotas, teams work together as a group to seize market opportunities. This fosters collaboration, innovation, sharing information and co-operation to bring in new business together. It avoids individuals being distracted by the need to protect themselves and their own self-promoting agenda.

Leaders must also make mutual understanding implicit in how everyone works with one another - that working together is a social contract with reciprocal requirements. A leader's ability to make the team accountable for success or failure, rather than individual success, increases trust and a sense of unity. However, this doesn't mean employees don't have individual goals. Instead, individual members establish a clear line of sight between their day-to-day responsibilities and the overarching, broader objectives of the organisation, as well as the over-arching team goals.

Most importantly, it also involves everyone taking ownership and credit when things go well – and badly. In a command-and-control hierarchy, typically the boss cops all of the flack while team members shirk responsibility. Today, a sense of ownership must become more evenly distributed. All it takes is the leader to transition team members from their safe, individualistic perspective to the collective. It's about instilling the mindset: *team success is not about smart individuals; it's about individuals working smarter together.*

A team is really all about combining strengths and using everyone's skills to complement one another. That's why we need to transition to team success being about teams winning together, rather than individuals.

> **In other words, high performance teams share a joint commitment to achieving the highest standards and the best results. Everyone is aligned to achieving the group goal.**

In team meetings, ensuring you reward behaviours that work towards a shared goal is important to reduce the negative impact of self-interested behaviours. Discourage individuals from trying to 'look good' by stressing the importance of interdependence as the key to success. When people do great work connect that to how it helps everyone – team members and customers.

Encourage speaking up

Humans are designed to avoid conflict. Employees fear speaking up about issues in case it makes them look stupid or unpopular. Having the courage to be vulnerable in a high stakes situation takes a lot of guts.

Being nimble and adaptive is a business requirement for success, but it will never occur in an organisation where people are afraid to raise issues. Addressing painful truths is the way to growth. After all, if you don't get the unpleasant stuff out of the way, you can waste a lot of time. It's hard to get moving on anything if people won't talk through issues or how to resolve them.

A 2016 study by VitalSmarts, a leadership training company, found that rather than talking about issues, employees were engaging in resource-sapping behaviours such as complaining to others (78%), doing extra or unnecessary work (66%), ruminating about the problem (53%), or getting angry (50%).

These are costly behaviours. The same research found that the average person wasted seven days undertaking these dysfunctional behaviours instead of talking about the problems. A shocking 40% of respondents admitted to wasting two weeks or more. Silence damages deadlines, budgets, relationships, turnover, employee engagement and meeting goals. If the culture is really toxic, high performers leave and leaders spend most of their time fixing people issues rather than actually working on strategy.

In his Harvard Business Review article, *Candour, Criticism and Teamwork*, Keith Ferrazzi researched executive teams at six top banks to gauge their level of candour. Teams that scored low on candour had the poorest financial returns among those banks during the global financial crisis. In contrast, teams that openly spoke about risky securities, lending practices and other potential problems were able to preserve shareholder value. In fact, further research by Ferrazzi into 50 large companies found that high performance could be predicted through identifying 'observable candour.'

STRATEGY 1: REDUCING INTERPERSONAL RISK

But the reason people don't speak up is not just because they don't feel safe, it's also because of the powerful magnetic pull of groupthink. Groupthink is when decision-making suffers as a group becomes insulated from dissenting viewpoints. Team members become so comfortable with one another that they are unaware of the subtle pressures to be unanimous in decisions.

Groupthink goes unnoticed because for many of us it is a safe and comfortable mode of operating. We go with what the group says because we don't want to seem disagreeable and risk being disliked.

It plays out with team members always agreeing with what is being said and being unable to raise uncomfortable issues. Rather than confront realities, leaders and team members shut down discourse about past mistakes. People are more keen to ensure the team is harmonious than to actually sort out disagreements that will cause larger issues later on. Blame, making excuses and a refusal to be responsible rule.

This is detrimental to an organisation because mistakes are seen as embarrassing rather than an opportunity to learn and improve. People are more concerned about protecting their own self-interests than finding solutions. They put limits on what's possible and their own capabilities.

It puts the organisation at risk of competitors out-innovating and taking customers. Every time an insight or question is withheld it means that the decision-making process is not as rigorous as it needs to be. As a leader you want to minimise this as much as possible.

For example, a CEO brought me in to work with her leadership team as there was conflict and a refusal to accept the new strategy. During a workshop I facilitated, the CEO shared her concerns with the team about speed decreasing and leaders not working together. Executives were clearly shocked and discussed why the CEO was incorrect. The good news was they were debating (and being aware of a new viewpoint), but the bad news was they were in serious denial about how their camaraderie was masking a lot of hidden issues that were frustrating many of them. It took some data, coaching and another workshop for them to come around and start being more open and honest.

Having worked with various executive teams, I have found the biggest stumbling block to understanding why things need to change is the pretence that things are perfect. It doesn't matter if the CEO or other managers in the business tell them the problem; senior executives wrongly assume that their ability to chat nicely together, or like one another, means that they are doing okay. Unfortunately, they are confusing talking at people as being the same as getting things done. The reality is, while leaders might appear to spend time talking, their dialogue is superficial and unproductive. Most are chronically unaware that they are withholding important information, avoiding accountability or conflict, not asking the right questions, acting defensively, accepting questionable strategies or offering few suggestions.

At the heart of it all, teams are under the spell of the compelling myth that communication is about talking (at people, or shouting, depending on the team dynamics). It's not. It's about productive dialogue around strategy and how to effectively co-ordinate requests and promises across an organisation.

> **This requires truth-seeking conversations that debate, challenge and get under the hood of important issues, in order to free up bottlenecks and reallocate resources.**

STRATEGY 1: REDUCING INTERPERSONAL RISK

Productive dialogue is difficult and requires the CEO to champion a psychologically safe space where members can talk candidly and honestly with one another. Leaders need to agree publicly on their commitments, suggest counteroffers when the work can't be done at the required time (or quality) or make plain refusals.

As a team leader, you need to be aware of the hypnotic pull of groupthink and the human tendency to not speak up about issues. This requires leading your team meetings to ensure that groupthink is reduced.

Best practice includes enabling equal turns in speaking for all who are present. This is much easier to do online. Keep a note of who has spoken and who hasn't. Ask those who have stayed quiet what they think. Ensure you don't allow only the loudest people to express their opinions.

If some people are still shy in speaking, reframe the risks of speaking up. We often hold back because we fear it's unsafe, but let people know that it's more risky to your team if they don't flag any issues with you. Let people know you want to act on any problems and take action as early as possible.

And don't be afraid of people not agreeing on a topic. Healthy debate is what is needed to reduce the tendency towards groupthink, and to really flesh out the feasibility of strategic initiatives or project tasks. Without robust discussion you get mediocre ideas and a lack of commitment.

But it's not just in meetings where we want people to use their voice. Empower employees to be able to ask questions about deadlines and to ask what the impact is if a deadline is pushed back. Allow employees to set their own boundaries and negotiate deadlines, so they don't feel overwhelmed by tasks. This is critical to stop people from operating in the anxiety zone.

Change how team members discuss and receive Issues

You know that you have a psychologically safe team when employees are respectful and feel obligated to be candid. They ask questions to ensure they understand a situation or perspective, they ask colleagues for help or their point of view and they openly admit if they are behind schedule.

Candour in the workplace is indeed shaped by leaders but it also requires every employee to demonstrate emotional maturity and discuss issues rather than complain about them. And to listen – to younger colleagues, customers, our peers and the little voice inside ourselves.

It starts with building team dynamics, so that everyone has the ability to question the status quo and challenge the leader. This also means employees listen to feedback that they receive from others, and that each employee knows how to provide feedback in a helpful and positive manner.

Model these behaviours by encouraging people to question or challenge your perspective. Answer difficult questions candidly and thank people for asking them. And stay calm – don't get defensive, embrace the opportunity to help people understand issues at a deeper level.

A simple, but powerful technique is to use the SSK feedback frame. It encourages your team to discuss issues honestly, counteracting the innate fear of speaking up. The specificity of the questions provides rich insights and anchors your team in reality.

The questions are:

- What should we **stop** doing?
- What should we **start** doing?
- What should we **keep** doing?

Ask these questions each week in your team meetings to encourage people to not only think differently about their work, but also to openly flag issues.

Best meeting practices to reduce interpersonal risk in your team

A great way to reduce interpersonal risk and to encourage team members to be interested in one another is to run meetings so that people feel safe. This isn't easy because a lot of leaders have bad habits that unintentionally make people feel unsafe.

You want to make sure that you ask questions in a way that enables people to feel heard, valued and appreciated. The objective here is to model candour, be respectful and teach people the importance of understanding each other and situations.

Here are some important tips to help you reduce team interpersonal risk (that also apply in your one-on-ones):

Welcome each person – Greet each person when they walk into the room or appear virtually. Make everyone feel welcome. Let people know you see them.

Listen, really listen – Listen more than you speak. I would guess that about 95% of people like to talk – about themselves. There is nothing more boring for people than going to a meeting and the boss spends 25 minutes talking, leaving five minutes at the end for discussion. This works against us when we are trying to make others feel safe. Give people space to talk. Demonstrate you are listening by clarifying or validating what they said. For example, 'I just want to make sure I understood that. Did you mean…?' or, 'It sounds like you feel overwhelmed. Is that correct?' When people finish talking ask, 'Is there anything else you want to add?' or, 'Is there something else you wanted to discuss that we missed?'

Give eye contact – Make sure you are really present when someone is talking. Avoid looking over their shoulder or glancing at your phone. Look into the other person's eyes, taking into account their reaction. If they keep looking away, reduce eye contact. This is respectful towards those who feel uncomfortable with eye contact. If they hold your gaze for a good period of time, keep up regular contact.

Take action, if required – If someone flags an issue that needs attention, make sure you do something about it. Ignoring issues generates distrust. At a later time, follow up with progress or resolutions to ensure people know that you value their contribution.

Say thanks – Avoid the tendency to either gloss over what is hard for people to share or dismiss what is uncomfortable for you. During these times, it's even more important to really listen and ask for more information. Let people know that you appreciate their comments or opinions. Providing thanks encourages safety and increases the likelihood that people will flag issues when they pop up.

Admit what you don't know – Flagging that you don't know something can almost visibly help people relax. Asking questions is also an opportunity to confess you don't know something. People are more likely to help us when we ask for their advice. This signals to people that you are there for them, not for yourself.

Don't interrupt – It goes without saying that it's important to listen to what people say, yet this can be remarkably hard for some leaders. Avoid talking over people or even answering the question for them.

Keep your body language open – Ensure your body language shows your interest in what people are saying. Keep your arms open; don't cross them. Make sure your body is facing them rather than the door or wherever you really want to be.

Observe people's facial expression and body language – Take note when people grimace or act defensive. This is your cue to change your wording, lean in closer and find out what is bugging them. You will know when you're getting this right, when team members check in with each other.

Repeat the same questions weekly – The more you ask people the same question, the better their responses get. Expect answer quality to be pretty low in the first few weeks, but as you consistently ask the same ones, your employees will expect them and prepare an answer. This helps improve their self-reflection and work quality.

Reflection

- When do you tend to ignore what people are saying? Are there certain times when you avoid hearing uncomfortable information?
- What techniques can you incorporate in your meetings to ensure they are safe and engaging?
- How can you modify your non-verbal communication?

Strategy 2:
Showing Support

*"People don't care how much you know,
until they know how much you care"*

American author and leadership expert – John C Maxwell

Leaders who care, get the most out of their people. Essentially, humans don't trust people who don't care about them.

According to neuroscience, the reward network in our brain is activated not only when we give support, but also when we receive it. Support reduces the threat of interpersonal risk. We feel safe because we know we aren't alone.

When we care for one another, it produces emotional safety.

Showing support is really about helping people become the best version of themselves. This encompasses providing guidance on doing excellent work and also on how to be a better human being. A great leader models and teaches how to treat people well, be of service, consider others and enjoy life.

According to 2012 research by Christina Boedker from the Australian School of Business, of all of the various measurements her research team looked at in an organisation, it was, the ability of the leader to be compassionate that had the greatest correlation with profitability and productivity. Her definition of being compassionate in this context is 'to understand people's motivators, hopes and difficulties and to create the right support mechanism to allow people to be as good as they can be'.

There is a number of things you can do to support your team, from communicating with compassion to setting clear expectations, getting out of their way to praising their achievements. Let's take a look.

Use inclusive language

Leaders need to ensure team members feel supported by them and everyone else in their team. A technique that works towards this is using inclusive language. Avoid using too many 'I' statements and focus on more 'we' statements. Sprinkling your languages with words such as 'everyone', 'together', 'all of us', 'team' and 'teammates' helps people feel part of the team. Consider using phrases such as 'we are listening' or 'we want to share' to better convey that leadership also cares about employees.

Communicate with emotional resonance

Remember that trust is an emotion that we process in our limbic brain that has no capacity for language. We trust people based on how they make us feel, rather than what they say. You can create a more supportive team environment by recognising and accepting peoples' emotions as part of daily work life.

It can be as simple as starting meetings encouraging people to express how they are feeling. One method is to observe how people look and then enquire. For example, asking 'Hey Melanie, you look happy and relaxed. What is making your upbeat?' or 'Hey Scott, you look stressed. What's happening in your world?'

Leaving our emotions, or humanness, at the office door is not appropriate or healthy. It isn't even possible when everyone can see into your personal life in an online meeting. It stands to reason that when people turn up to work each day, so do their personal struggles.

Sharing emotions is important for our brain to relax, trust the situation and commit to achieving goals.

In some ways, COVID has been a gift to understand people's situation and to care more about how others are feeling because during these difficult times people feel more vulnerable than before. It's opened our hearts. And now we have the opportunity to continue to open them by not making the personality delineation between being at work or home.

Another technique to improve the emotional intelligence (understanding your own and others' emotions and how they drive behaviour, to then motivate others) of your team is replacing the question, 'What do you *think* about this?' with, 'How do you *feel* about this?'. Our feelings unlock solutions that provide far deeper insights than our surface thoughts (or what we think people want us to say). It also gets us thinking more about outcomes, rather than tasks.

Build stronger relationships

Ask people about what is going on in their personal lives. Regularly ask questions about their family or interests that show you care and see them as more than just a productivity tool. If you've got a really good memory, you can score extra points if you can remember people's family or pet names.

Don't be afraid to take the time for each team member to share what's going on in their lives. Creating opportunities for people to learn about each other outside of work is important. Make sure that you schedule social time before or after a meeting to allow people to talk about their personal lives. You can even have virtual coffee or lunches, where people chat over meals. Help team members understand one another in terms of their dreams, fears, values, challenges and goals.

Understanding people ensures that you can talk into what they are experiencing rather than defaulting into 'business as usual' language. It also makes you more relatable.

Set clear expectations and timelines

One of the downsides of building close work relationships is that your direct reports may take advantage of you.

Social exchange theory suggests that managers and employees interact through repeated give-and-take transactions. There is an exchange of resources such as work effort, guidance and rewards, and these interactions shape the quality of the relationship. Over time, if the employee can be trusted to deliver high quality work they are rewarded with more assignments, more meaningful work and recognition. Typically, employees then return the favour immediately by being keen to deliver to a high standard.

A 2018 field study by Zhenyu Liao from Washington University found that how much managers and employees 'give and take' fluctuated considerably across interactions. When managers gave more in a certain interactions, employees immediately felt obligated to 'repay' them by putting in more work effort and contributing more next time.

STRATEGY 2: SHOWING SUPPORT

However, this wasn't true with employees who had stronger working relationships with their managers. They were less likely to reciprocate the favour right away or even at all. The study concluded that these employees seemed to take advantage of the good rapport they had with their boss, making reciprocation unbalanced in the short term.

The implication is that managers who believe that their employees will do the right thing by them because the working relationship is strong face an unexpected risk. Their employees will actually be more likely to let them down by not fulfilling immediate requests. This can be quite devastating to well-meaning leaders, who can feel betrayed.

The researchers surmised that it's still important to build strong relationships with employees, as the benefits still outweigh the issues. However, don't assume that because you have a strong relationship that your employee will do the right thing. If anything, it becomes more important to set clear expectations and timelines. You want to make sure that your direct reports know what is urgent, how to prioritise it and what good looks like. Otherwise, they are more likely to focus on other tasks. A strong relationship gives them a false sense of security that they can do work in their own time.

> **When expectation doesn't meet reality, you have distrust.**

The main takeout here is to always be clear on timelines, goals and expectations, and to not change them. People go into fear when they are not sure of what is required and fall into disengagement when their job is confusing. Building a trusting environment requires setting clear goals and expectations.

Remove roadblocks

Demonstrate that you care about your employees by removing barriers and bottlenecks so people can do their best work in service of a shared goal.

When a manager doesn't understand that sometimes goals can't be met, it shows a lack of empathy. It puts people offside when they've worked hard to reach a goal.

Your role is to empower people to do their best work. Provide your team with the right resources, tools, decisions and training.

Regularly ask: 'How's your project going? What's working? What's not? How can I help?'

Sometimes you might be the blocker, holding things up. If another team is gumming up the works by not delivering, be a true ally to your team and get out there, talk to the team leader and sort out the issue. Doing what you can to demonstrate that you are on your team's side ensures that you are regarded as a trusted leader.

Provide autonomy

The happiest people I interview in companies are those given the freedom to choose how, when and where they work. Encourage people to work when they are most productive. That could be really early in the morning or late at night. Just make sure they are still held accountable for results and have the right competencies to complete the task. Empower power people to master their tasks their way.

Provide praise

We probably don't recognise people for doing good work as much as we think we do. Recognising and rewarding employees for their work is critical for high trust workplaces. Employees need to feel like they are accomplishing outcomes and making progress.

Praising people's work validates their effort and what's important to you. There are lots of creative ways you can reward people. According to Dr Paul Zak, in his book *The Trust Factor*, a rule of thumb is to ensure it occurs within a week after completing the task well.

Ideally, you also thank people individually first. This gives you the opportunity to ensure they are okay with being publicly recognised, not everyone is. However, recognising people, collectively, in a team meeting is ideal. It reinforces teamwork and helps motivate team members. Verbal thanks is often all that you need, but you can amp it up with a small gift card if you have available budget.

And be specific with your praise. A good technique to encourage learning in your team is to articulate how the goal was met or the problem solved. This ensures that you are focusing on continuous improvement (which I talk about more in the next section).

In addition to providing regular positive feedback, celebrate wins and milestones.

Supporting your direct reports is all about removing barriers, cheering them on, boosting their confidence, coaching them or getting our of their way. The more people grow their capabilities, the more confident they become. And it starts with creating a supportive environment where they know they can make mistakes and still be accepted by you and the team.

Reflection

- How can you remove roadblocks that are frustrating your people and slowing down work?
- What can you do to increase people's autonomy in their roles?
- How do you verbally recognise people? Do you praise them in terms of their individual capabilities or success or do you link it to how it helps the team?

Strategy 3.
Fostering Learning

"Organisations learn only through individuals who learn."
– American systems scientist Peter Senge

The need for ongoing learning is greater now than at any other time in history. With the immense rate of change in today's business landscape, the shelf life of skills is decreasing, putting pressure on employees to continue learning.

One of the benefits of psychological safety is that it creates an environment where people are willing to learn. Psychological safety enables people to go outside of their comfort zone and learn new things. According to a 1999 study by Dr Amy Edmondson, it also encourages people to engage in learning behaviours such as sharing information, asking for help or experimenting.

Learning supports people in reaching their potential and feeling that the organisation cares about them. We are more likely to adapt to change in a culture where learning from mistakes is rewarded and indeed, celebrated.

When mistakes are seen as bad rather than as learning opportunities, people are likely to fall into 'learning anxiety' where they become defensive if things don't go as well as they expected. In fact, a 1993 study by Schein found that fear inhibits learning. Fear diverts mental resources to the parts of the brain that manage working memory and process new information, impairing our analytical thinking, creative insight and problem solving.

We can't learn if we don't feel safe. Yet, there is one catch.

It has been estimated that only 10% of the population has a learning mindset. These are people who actively seek out and enjoy learning. The other 90% will not improve their skills unless they have to as part of their job requirement. Some employees actively resist continuous learning or rely on their manager to determine the skills they require on their career path.

As a leader, you want to take your direct reports on a journey where you are all learning together, where learning is safe and protective. You want to learn forward. Not only does this increase safety, but it also improves people's confidence and competencies.

This requires embedding learning into your day-to-day activities so that personal growth is everyone's job, not a separate task that you do when you have time. It's about having learning conversations during regular interactions with your team. It requires leading from the perspective of 'How can I help my people grow?'

Learning forward as a team enables employees to expand their abilities. It creates a wonderful virtuous cycle where employees learn, try something new and receive positive results, which boosts their motivation and confidence to continue. It is how teams sustain being in the achievement zone long term.

STRATEGY 3. FOSTERING LEARNING

Learning reverses the negative impact of a vicious cycle where people feel uncertain and fearful, fail to get results, lose their confidence and then refuse to try anything new.

So it is important to create the right learning environment. Here are some approaches you can take to do this.

Embrace errors

How you deal with wins and losses in your team will dictate how safe people feel to learn. Reframe errors as learning opportunities so that new tactics and best practices are quickly developed. Understand that projects or concepts fail, not people. This requires having an inquisitive mind and asking curious questions that do not assign blame. Use 'what' or 'how' questions such as, 'What's worked?' or, 'How can we improve this for next time?'. Avoid 'why' questions such as, 'Why did you do that?', which makes people defensive and likely to shut down.

Focus on growing people

Work with your employees to understand their career aspirations. Engage with people through their individual career paths by asking where they want to be in five years' time and what skills they need so you can help match them to new tasks. Be willing to help employees understand their strengths and weaknesses.

Promote learning opportunities

Employees will learn more if it is easy to do so or required in their daily work activities. Advocate access to on-demand online learning, so employees can learn whenever and wherever they want. Regularly inform employees of training and development opportunities in the organisation. Ensure there is training available to all, not just 'high potentials'.

Encourage group learning

Explicitly embed learning time into every team meeting. In your team meeting agenda, assign learning time. You can mix it up as well. One week you can share three positives and negatives about a recent work project. The next week you can get employees to share their non-work expertise such as sharing their volunteer experience or things they have learned at a training course. The week after that you could encourage team members to share their client learnings.

Ensure personal development is employee led, not manager led

It is not up to you to manage people's personal development. Empower your employees to discover what interests them and what they wish to learn, so they make their own learning and career choices. Help employees transition from the mindset that managers must lead their personal development to the mindset that they must lead it.

Reflection

- Underpinning a learning forward culture is a leader who embraces the concept of becoming a lifelong learner. How are you constantly learning new things and modelling that to your team members?

- Improving your abilities isn't only about what you learn, it's about balancing both external learning and internal learning (looking within). Journalling, working with a coach or therapist or doing meditation can help. What steps can you take to learn more about yourself?

- Leaders in the achievement zone are passionate about learning and trying new things. What can you do to be more curious?. What new thing can you try out? It could be learning a new language, driving a different way to work or trying a new food.

Summary: Fostering Safety

Trusting others is a key component of being human. The relationships we have that make us feel safe are really important to us.

There are three strategies to improve safety:

Strategy 1: Reduce Interpersonal Risk

Most negative employee behaviours stem from a subconscious fear of being kicked out of the team. Understand that when employees act negatively it is to protect themselves (not be a pain in the neck for the sake of it).

Strategy 2: Show Support

Empower people to do their best work. Support your employees in their career or personal goals, remove roadblocks and provide resources.

Strategy 3: Foster Learning

As a leader, you want to take your direct reports on a journey where you are all learning together. Learning is safe and protective. Not only does this increase safety, but it also improves people's confidence and competencies.

Key Interaction: Meetings and One-on-Ones

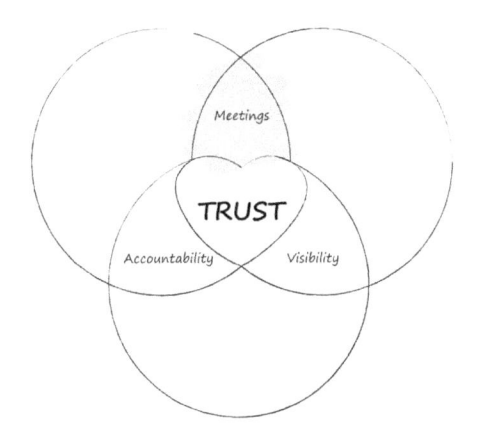

In the *Integrated Trust Building System*, at the intersection between *safety* and *connection* is *meetings*. Any business relationship is a social contract between one or more people; being clear about mutual expectations is important to ensure shared understanding of work and behaviours. It's all about consultation and having regular two-way dialogue. It's not about talking at people but taking the time to understand their viewpoint so that they feel included in decisions. Otherwise, you run the risk of people pulling back.

Effective meetings and one-on-ones

> *"The single biggest problem in communication is the illusion it has taken place."*
>
> George Bernard Shaw

Humans need certainty and communication is all about reducing ambiguity. Without it, we tend to not trust a situation becoming fearful.

A critical role of a manager or team leader is to look for ways to make things truly better in your department. Every hour of your day should be spent increasing the output or the value of the output of the people you're responsible for.

As Andy Grove said in his iconic book *High Output Management*, your productivity as a manager is the productivity of your team. Grove called this managerial leverage – the impact of what managers do to increase the output of their teams.

Essentially, high managerial productivity is a combination of choosing to perform tasks that possess high leverage and elicit peak performance from the individuals within the team.

Meetings and one-on-ones are both high leverage activities for team leaders. The more time you invest in building close relationships, the more invested your team will be in both you and the organisation. This works towards helping you more effectively gain and share information, make decisions, influence others and model core workplace behaviours.

While meetings and one-on-ones take time to prepare for and run, long term they save you time and enable your team to work faster and cohesively. Meetings help you build stronger connections between teammates, while one-on-ones helps you form close bonds to your direct reports. Both techniques work towards reducing any perceived threats employees feel in a workplace that might subconsciously encourage them to pull back their full commitment.

You are constantly being watched by your direct reports. They look to you as to what behaviours are acceptable in the organisation, for clues on how to best work with you and for evidence that you model the company values.

> **One of the biggest complaints I hear from employees in stakeholder interviews are that leaders aren't 'walking the talk'.**

Employees want to see leaders match their words to their actions. In particular, they want to see them practising the company values and facing consequences when they don't take values seriously. Essentially, people want to see evidence that the organisation and leaders care about people. And they need to feel it through observing how leaders interact and treat people during discussions.

Let's take a look at how to harness the power of two-way dialogue in these important modes:

Meetings

According to a 2015 Gallup Study, employees whose managers hold regular meetings with them are almost three times as likely to be engaged as employees whose managers do not hold regular meetings with them. Regular interactions with people are critical for building trust and team cohesiveness.

Meeting face-to-face is an obvious method to build trust. Research by Alex Pentland, in *The New Science of Building Great Teams* found that it is because it increases the number and nature of exchanges between team members. While face-to-face is not possible for those working from home or located across different regions, having daily or weekly virtual meetings clears roadblocks and helps people get clarity and focus on the right priorities. Virtual meetings are still good for building trust but the impact decreases the more people that you have online.

If you have a large team meeting of more than 20 people, you will want to split them into sub-groups of two to three people and then reconvene to talk to everyone. This will ensure that people feel safer in sharing their concerns and brainstorming new ideas. Not everyone feels comfortable expressing their viewpoints in front of a large group, and the tendency will be to resort to email where confusion and frustrations reign.

Often, leaders tell me they stopped calling meetings because they waste time. Yes, meetings can be a total waste of time when leaders aren't any good at running them!

Failing to schedule regular meetings means leaders are in constant fire-fighting mode dealing with lots of little issues throughout the day. The irony is that if they had a consistent communication rhythm these issues would be cleared at once, freeing up time.

> **Show me a leader who refuses to have regular meetings and I'll show you a leader whose direct reports don't trust them.**

Leaders who have mastered how to run meetings effectively are more connected and present to the challenges facing the business.

This builds an important intuitive feel for the organisation and the people in it. It's also a powerful connection tool that links everyone to you and each other. Helping people feel that you trust them.

But they do take time to get right. You must set aside time to clearly think and plan how to do them. And respect people's time. This is critical because in the age of working from home Zoom fatigue can be a real problem. Making meetings shorter and only inviting those who really need to be there is important to ensuring people aren't being overwhelmed.

It's also important to empower employees to have the right to disconnect – to be able to decline a meeting if they haven't seen an agenda or if the agenda isn't a fit.

What people really want to know is what they need to do, how they need to do it, when, why and for whom. In other words, they want clarity around decision-making, directives, expectations, deadlines all combined with regular feedback loops. Without the right context, people fear they will disappoint their boss or their job is at risk. They get confused and stuck. They focus on the wrong tasks. And they feel disconnected, unsafe and unsettled.

The best team meetings have routines and regular questions that reinforce the right behaviours, helping people to know what to expect. They also clarify how everything works together across the organisation and are an important opportunity to increase inclusivity and consultation. Particularly, with other teams throughout the firm.

The real litmus test of a successful meeting is that they are energising. Even if the workload is overwhelming or a new idea is presented – a good meeting provides clarity, alignment and a path forward. They keep organisations healthy. Whereas a poor meeting makes people feel drained, 'bashed up' or frustrated that they lost important time to do other work.

One-on-ones

While meetings are great to unite the team, one-on-ones are critical to improving individual performance. It is where you effectively become a coach and accountability partner to each of your reports, demonstrating that you really care about your employees and helping them navigate both their personal and work lives.

You do this through really listening to what people have to say, being curious and excited about their responses and tying back what they say to their goals, both personal and professional.

The aim of one-on-ones is to enable you to have honest conversations with your direct reports so you can flag performance and behavioural issues without any resistance – all in the spirit of helping them grow. You provide guidance when their performance goes off track and align them to the vision. One-on-ones also allow you to you clear up any confusion, so that they are working on the right things.

In the age of remote work, one-on-ones reduce the potential for misunderstandings and create rapport. Our innate threat detector is always on the lookout for any perceived threats; one-on-ones help both of you understand and read each other's non-verbal signals. This is critical as it bonds you together as fellow team members and not a threat. They also make direct reports feel more connected to not only their leader, but the organisation as a whole.

Best practice for remote employees is a slightly longer run time on one-on-ones. Working remotely can increase feelings of isolation, so schedule more time so they can ask more questions, feel clear about what they're doing and connected to you.

Essentially, you want to be consistent in letting people know that they matter and belong – that their skills and abilities makes a difference.

Importantly, one-on-ones benefit you enormously. As Andy Grove said in *The High-Output Manager*, the main purpose of the one-on-one is exchanging information and mutual education. By discussing specific problems and situations, the supervisor teaches their direct report decision-making and problem solving skills and the best way to approach issues. Simultaneously, the team member provides detailed information about what they are doing and their concerns. It increases autonomy and sense of mastery, reducing dependency on you.

A further advantage of one-on-ones is that it shifts from performance management to performance development.

A 2015 study by Right Management found that two-thirds of the factors that motivate performance at work are tied to career conversations and development opportunities. Rather than doing standard six month or annual performance reviews, companies that train managers to deliver career conversations and development opportunities more effectively have 29% higher revenue, lower turnover and talent acquisition costs, and stronger customer loyalty. Yet, 68% of managers are not engaged in their team's development.

The problem is annual performance evaluations are often too late and send the wrong messages to everyone about performance improvement. The reality is that accumulating feedback over time is not only irrelevant, but it's overwhelming and unfair. It is also administration heavy and doesn't improve performance.

Not only that, managers hate doing performance reviews. Conversations are often forced and superficial. And it's made worse if employees do not clearly understand their goals or what is expected of them at work. One-on-ones get around these issues because they are friendly, regular conversations that ensure no-one is caught unaware with performance issues.

While shifting from performance management to performance development has been a trend for a while, few companies have made it work. According to Michael Kim (head of HR at Spotify) who was speaking at a conference in Melbourne in 2019, this is because 'It's more than a shift in semantics. It's a total shift in mindset.'

At Spotify, they are getting better results from managers being taught how to have regular one-on-ones rather than waste time undertaking annual performance reviews. It also means giving managers who work directly with their people the authority to grant a pay rise, rather than head office.

Spotify realise this mindset shift involves leaders understanding that trust is at the centre. Leaders have to build a level of trust with their people. And you can't do that if you are collecting issues about your employees and then dumping on them twice annually.

And one further thing – when you book one-on-one meetings, avoid cancelling them because it causes a lot of trust issues. In one organisation I worked with, the team leader would regularly cancel one-on-one meetings. The excuse was that they had to do urgent work for the senior leadership team, but all that did was tell team members that senior leaders were more important than them.

To ensure you run efficient one-on-one meetings, encourage your direct report to write an agenda for you both. They need to take ownership of the get-together – all you need is clarity and some good questions to get them thinking.

Here are some helpful questions to play around with:

What do you like doing outside of work? – Checking in with someone personally is a great way to start. Best practice is to spend at least five minutes about personal stuff to build connection. It sends the message that you care about your direct report and don't just see them as someone who does tasks for you. This question shows your interest in them, but it can also help you link what they like doing to job tasks. For example, I coached a team leader who loved to run business events outside of work. The reason he did this was because he liked being a host and helping strangers connect and learn about one another. His boss was able to leverage this information to set him up to run successful customer events.

What motivates you to come to work? – This is a great emotional check-in to open the gateway to richer conversations, so that people are more comfortable flagging any personal or mental health issues. It also taps into people discussing their feelings to help open up greater insights about themselves.

How happy are you with your performance? What would you improve? –This question encourages honesty and self-reflection. It also gives you powerful information on how to support them.

The power of active questions

> *"You can tell whether a man is clever by his answers.*
> *You can tell whether a man is wise by his questions."*
>
> Naguib Mahfouz – Egyptian novelist and Nobel laureate

The core to leveraging face-to-face time (both virtual and in-person) is the art of asking great questions; one of my favourite leadership tools to foster high impact conversations.

Robert Bales, one of the first scientists to study group communications, discovered that while questions comprise only 6% of verbal interactions, they generate 60% of subsequent discussions.

The benefits of running meetings through asking incisive questions are countless. First of all, it ensures that you stay present, which makes others feel heard and valued. You also receive important feedback about where people are at and their level of awareness of an issue, which helps you make more informed decisions.

Incisive questions also encourage others to generate new ways of thinking or looking at an issue, rather than the fairly typical practice of people advocating or agreeing that often leads to groupthink.

Asking questions also helps team members form bonds with one another, as they listen to one another's issues and progress. It fosters commitment and passion in staff that makes them more likely to follow you during change and uncertainty. It also ensures meetings are far more engaging and avoids you spending all your time talking.

Not only that, questions focus people's attention on what truly matters. And they can be used to take people on 'quests', or mental journeys, in search of answers.

As James Kouzes and Barry Posner explained in their book *The Leadership Challenge*, the questions that a leader asks send messages about the focus of the organisation. They indicate what is of most concern to the leader (and what each direct report also needs to monitor).

> ***Every question is a potential learning opportunity.***

It's less about being directive and more about being inquisitive. Ask questions such as, 'What excites you about this new project? What help do you need from me to get started?'

It also trains people to ask other team member's questions (an indicator of high performing teams), which reduces time wasted through people trying to work it out themselves or pretending they know the answer. Furthermore, it creates the necessity for voice, ensuring that people avoid staying quiet for fear of retribution. It sends the subtle message that people's voices are important because you are expecting an answer.

The more your subordinates get used to being asked questions, the more likely they will be to stop requiring excessive direction and approval. They stop being order-takers that do what they are told and start figuring out things on their own. They gain the confidence to trust themselves to solve problems and take the initiative. And their answers get better over time.

One of the challenges with being a leader is avoiding the belief that you have to have all the answers. There are so many unknowns and so much uncertainty. Leading by asking questions models to your direct reports that even during a crisis, you can calmly address an issue through asking deep questions and keeping the lines of communication open.

Think of leading your team as being like a cool DJ at a nightclub who seamlessly mixes in a new song to the beat of the current track, expertly adjusting and blending the right content to shape the energy and vibrancy in a room, so that people move in sync with each other.

Learning to have genuine conversations that build human connection ensures that your direct reports feel supported. They're more likely to move out of their comfort zone into the achievement zone, working with others to be their best.

> **Remember, when it comes to reducing interpersonal risk, how we communicate is more important than what we communicate. This requires the leader to model these behaviours to encourage positive social interactions.**

Reflection

- In what circumstances do you feel you must have all the answers? What do you fear are the consequences if you don't know something? Is that really true?

- How frequently do you admit you don't know something? If it is less than weekly, a good habit is to say, 'I don't know the answer. What do you think?' Or, 'I need help with this. I've heard you're the person who knows what to do. What would you suggest?'

- How often do you apologise for mistakes and admit you were wrong? If it is rare, a good habit is to say, 'I stuffed that up. Sorry about that.'

- How do you encourage team members to listen to each other and receive feedback? A good technique is to model collaborative behaviours through asking team members after they disclose information, 'Is there anything else you'd like to add?' or 'That sounds like a difficult experience. Do you need further support from us?'

- How do you react to negative information? What ways can you make it safer for people to share errors?

Implementation

Add questions to your meeting agenda. Ideally, you ask these every week to make these habits a tradition. The goal here is to reduce interpersonal risk, focus on collective results, encourage speaking up and improve team member interactions. Some helpful examples include:

What new thing did you learn this week? – Embed learning into every team meeting. Ideally, learning is around understanding one another better, sharing best practices or industry trends. It's about increasing the energy of your team through exploring new territory.

What's your biggest frustration at work right now? – This is a great reflective question that helps people openly discuss issues. It reduces groupthink and increases alignment, ensuring that people are more likely to speak up and talk about problems, rather than being fearful about telling the truth.

What is working well in our team? What is not working well in our team? – These questions are useful to get deep into any dependency or interaction issues. They also tap into both negative and positive emotions to ensure people are willing to be vulnerable and it stops the positivity bias that all is well.

Case Study: Putting Fostering Safety Into Practice

Lauren is a chief financial officer in a medium sized engineering company. She contacted me about moving her team that were in apathy into the achievement zone. She had inherited the team from her predecessor; a mature, technically-oriented boss who preferred doing the work himself rather than delegating to his employees. The team were used to doing work at an average standard then leaving it to their boss to fix. They were given no clear expectations, autonomy, training or incentives to improve their work quality or make decisions. They were often quite fearful of their boss's moods and were frequently on sick leave.

Lauren had been brought in because she was more progressive and had a track record of navigating the finances of a growing company. Her mandate was to provide the board and CEO with more timely and appropriate financial reports using the current financial system, which the previous CFO had eschewed. But when she started working with her team, she realised they were frightened and overwhelmed by using the current financial software.

To improve the performance of her team, I introduced a two-pronged approach. The first one was to coach Lauren on how to create safety in her team. She started with doing fortnightly one-on-ones with each team member to encourage them to learn new things and feel supported by her, in order to improve their deliverables. She also introduced weekly team meetings with a clear agenda that encouraged team members to contribute. The previous CFO had refused to do team meetings, he considered them a waste of time because his finance team members didn't speak in meetings and the tasks never changed. I also coached Lauren on some best practices to facilitate fortnightly training sessions in a safe environment.

Case Study...

The second part of the approach was a workshop to help the financial team connect to the real purpose of their work and understand how they were of service to the whole organisation. We created a team expectations document so they could freely describe what behaviours they needed to feel safe – from their new boss and each other. Team members left energised with a renewed passion for their jobs.

Three months later, there was a stark improvement. Financial reports were being delivered on time to the board and CEO, rather than being late by 30 days. Some team members had stepped up and taken on tasks that they had been afraid of doing only months before. Productivity had improved by a huge 43% as the time taken to do tasks had been vastly improved and errors in work dropped by 67%. Not only that, sick days had been reduced by an astonishing 75%.

Even sitting in with the team was a different experience than with the previous CFO. Employees were animated, asked questions and were proud of their work. They were even keen to take work off the CFO's plate. When I asked Lauren how the team was going, she said, 'Before we started working together, I was really regretting taking on this role. It seemed too hard to improve the financials with a team that had been together for more than a decade. I didn't know how I was going to build their trust and motivation. But through regular coaching, asking questions and focusing on learning together, the whole vibe of the team has change. And the CEO is thrilled that he gets his reports on time and can quickly act on what's going on in the business.'

Practice 2:
Creating Connection

How to connect how everything links together

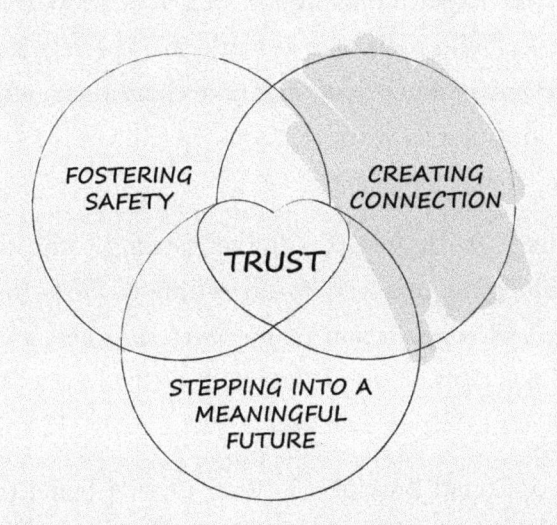

- FOSTERING SAFETY
- CREATING CONNECTION
- TRUST
- STEPPING INTO A MEANINGFUL FUTURE

We are biologically wired to want to be with other people. It is a deep human need to feel we belong that's fundamental to human motivation.

Connection is when we feel a sense of belonging to others in our team or workplace. This is deeper than just participating in a team, it is a feeling that arises when we believe we have high quality and meaningful social connections. In other words, connection is when relationships are more than just transactional.

Neuroscience experiments by Dr Paul Zak show that when people intentionally build social ties at work, their performance improves. When people know they belong and have the support when they need it, they have meaningful work relationships and feel more secure and loyal to their group.

A 2019 study by BetterUp, a digital learning company, found that workplace belonging can lead to an estimated 56% increase in job performance, a 50% reduction in turnover risk, and a 75% decrease in employee sick days. If you calculate the costs for a 10,000-person company, the annual savings would be more than $52 million.

Feeling connected provides us with myriad benefits. It helps us feel needed, that our contributions are valued and worthwhile and our beliefs are valid.

Not surprisingly, ostracism is one of our greatest fears. A 2003 study by Matthew Lieberman from the University of California found that social rejection activates many of the same brain regions involved in physical pain. Being alone can negatively affect our emotional state,

PRACTICE 2: CREATING CONNECTION

causing us to feel depressed, jealous, anxious or even violent towards other people. According to a 2010 Brigham Young University study, people with stronger social relationships have a 50% increased likelihood of living longer than those with weaker social relationships.

> *When we are surrounded by other people, we feel more alive than when we are alone.*

But up until fairly recently, feeling some sort of connection to teammates or the organisation wasn't something commonly acknowledged in business. In a workplace, there has been an uneasy tension between focusing on tasks and not wasting time making friends.

The pandemic has been a game changer in terms of our sense of belonging. Research by global thinktank Coqual found that belonging scores at workplaces shot up because employees recognised in a crisis that things weren't perfect. They gave their organisation slack as it scrambled to find new ways to support employees. The result was that workers could see that their organisations were trying to do the right thing, which increased loyalty and connection to their organisation. The phrase 'we're all in this together' uplifted and galvanised employees during uncertainty.

When connection is strained in an organisation, you can easily see it by simply walking around and noting the types of interactions. In the old days, this was simply observing whether people were talking to one another in the hallways and tearoom. Now, in a hybrid world of on-site and at-home work, it's seeing how many conversations are occurring on digital conversation channels.

Without connection, people don't have open conversations where they can talk through issues and remove bottlenecks. It slows down progress and makes the work of leaders much more frustrating and burdensome.

Feeling connected to our team makes us feel really good. But it doesn't happen on its own. It takes time and commitment. We have to make ourselves talk to people we don't like, uncover and accept differing perspectives and resolve conflicts.

Making the time to build connection with your direct reports might seem like a lot of work. And it can be. But it can actually become an enjoyable part of your job that creates less work long term.

When a leader puts the interests and wellbeing of their employees above their own, they become a trusted leader, one who is followed in a heartbeat during bad and good times.

The Challenges with Connection

The need for connection has a big impact on our happiness. Humans are fundamentally social. Many of us devote a lot of time and energy to relationships that are toxic. We seek approval from people who will never validate us, we try to make friends with leaders we revere only to discover they are not really that admirable, and we hang out with people who are self-absorbed and don't live our values.

Not only that, when we do make genuine connections to others, the sheer force of our will comes into play. We become defensive when our values, viewpoints or work are questioned. We feel hurt when a decision is made that doesn't suit us.

When we get really busy or stressed, we disconnect from others, preferring the comfort of our work to people. We pull away – either amplifying our own alienation or that of others.

PRACTICE 2: CREATING CONNECTION

It's important to understand that when your employees detach from the team it can flag that personal or work issues are getting them down. This is when you need to spend more time with them finding out how you can support them. And if you notice you are disengaging from those around you, then you need to spend time evaluating what is creating your need to separate. Sometimes working with a therapist or coach is helpful in these situations.

Connecting the Pieces

Workplaces tend to have lots of interdependencies, complexity and unknowns that change daily. High achievement leaders provide their team with contextual understanding of their work environment, which is critical for the speed and efficiency of their team.

Creating connection and a sense of belonging in a workplace is a multi-faceted process that is a bit like a jigsaw puzzle. Your role is to help 'connect the dots for people'. It's not just about connecting people to people, but also explaining how all of the different parts fit together within the broader landscape. From projects, products and platforms right through to all of the people that make everything happen. This works towards providing shared consciousness – a quality of high performing teams. It requires linking people to how their work impacts others, both within and outside your team.

When there is a lack of common or shared understanding within an organisation, it creates a whole raft of issues. These include:

- confusion around accountabilities and priorities,
- slow decision-making,
- constraints in the ability of teams to help other teams (silos).

As the team leader, your CEO and leadership team, expect you to focus your connection efforts on three areas (even if they don't know what they are specifically). These are:

- personal impact,
- beneficiaries,
- people and pieces.

Let's dive into these in more detail.

Strategy 1:
Linking Personal Impact

Story has it that when President John F Kennedy was visiting the NASA space centre in 1962, he noticed a janitor mopping the floor. He walked over to the man and said, 'Hi, I'm Jack Kennedy. What are you doing?'

'Well, Mr President,' the janitor responded, 'I'm helping put a man on the moon.'

You could be forgiven for thinking that the cleaner's remark was unique, given that his everyday work seemed light years away from achieving that famous goal. But across the 400,000-person organisation, other employees shared similar beliefs. NASA employees didn't define their work as 'I'm fixing electrical wiring' or 'I'm sewing space suits'. They associated their everyday tasks with 'I'm putting a man on the moon'.

> *Imagine what results your organisation could achieve if your employees were inspired and energised by the company vision.*

Whether we realise it or not, all of us are contributing to the larger story unfolding around us. It is the job of leadership to redefine work to help people see how they are contributing to a bigger picture. As leaders, we need to think about how we want our workforce to answer the question 'What are you doing?'

World-class organisations understand the importance of actively involving employees to achieve business goals, while at the same time communicating how each individual's contribution relates to the outcome. This is the secret behind improving intrinsic motivation.

It's your job to align each employee's self-interest to a more meaningful and bigger purpose set by the organisation. In other words, connecting employees to how their individual talents, values, interactions and effort makes a difference. The internal aspect of their work or personal effort and how it works towards building a better tomorrow.

As a leader, it's not enough to inspire ourselves and our team to complete work. The more we do work that appears to have no real purpose, the less motivated and engaged we become.

The Energy Project, a training and consultancy company, surveyed more than 12,000 employees across a range of companies and industries. They found a direct correlation between finding meaning in work and high performance.

The survey found that employees who claimed to derive meaning from their work were reportedly 1.4 times more engaged at work, 1.7 times more likely to feel job satisfaction and three times more likely to stay with their company. Unfortunately, only 50% of employees experienced a sense of meaning in their work.

A powerful leadership skill is to help employees understand the meaning of their role and how it contributes to the success of the organisation. Communications expert Bill Quirke is quoted as saying when employees understand their overall role in the business, 91% will work towards that success, but the number plummets to 23% if they don't.

STRATEGY 1: LINKING PERSONAL IMPACT

In a big organisation, it is easy for employees to lose their sense of identity and value when they are measured against the inner workings of the organisation and not their own potential.

Typically, leaders often discuss how strategies will move the company forward but fail to clarify how or why employees' contributions matter.

> **People need to know how their work connects to the organisation's vision and what's in it for them.**

Without a belief in personal impact, people tend to devalue their job. Work is transactional. Accountability is low. People feel replaceable. And while no leader or organisation can control meaningless, leaders can actively cause meaninglessness. A 2016 study reported in the Sloan Management Review found that few employees made any mention of effective leadership during meaningful moments at work. Yet, poor leadership was associated with undermining meaningfulness.

Successful leaders make an effort to ensure employees understand how their work makes a difference to the company. They can see the potential within their direct reports and help them to unlock that. The gap between an employee's values and the organisational values can lead to a deep sense of meaninglessness. After all, people want to feel that it matters if they turn up to work – that the work they do moves the needle on some metric for the company.

This is vital to transitioning your team into the achievement zone, rather than falling into the anxiety, abatement or apathy zones.

So how do you create a thriving workplace environment where people understand why their job matters? Let's go through some strategies to do this.

Have conversations on meaning

Humans are meaning-making machines. Despite our best intentions, we don't respond to actual situations and events. Instead, we respond to our interpretation of the event or the story we tell about ourselves about what happened.

In an uncertain world, our lives can change in an instant. We have little control over our circumstances. However, we can control the meaning we place on the situation.

> **As leaders, we can do this for our people by modelling flexible thinking and reframing the meaning behind events.**

In team meetings and one-on-ones, assist each team member to understand how they are uniquely contributing to the team's goals. Honest and transparent conversations help employees connect how their organisation makes the world a better place and their role within that.

The best way to do that is to ask questions that help people to self-reflect on their job role. After all, we don't often realise meaningfulness while we are at work. We tend to connect the dots when we reflect on our past work and what gives us joy and what doesn't.

Periodically stepping back and assessing work and actions ensures people are more present to creating a meaningful experience in their careers and making a bigger impact.

This also means highlighting that each employee is responsible for seeing the meaning within each task and committing to performing beyond an ordinary level. Openly discuss with your team members:

- What are we working on that is personally important?
- What's the point of the work we are doing?
- What can you do personally to ensure your work is making an impact for clients (no matter how small)?

These questions foster in-depth conversations that not only help each team member understand one another better, but also highlight that there are times when meaningful work is not enjoyable. It is only when we look back and reflect that we can see how a challenge enabled us to improve what we do. Not only that, sometimes our work connects to our personal and professional life. We might find that our contribution makes a difference to our friends or family.

Connect individual work to the big vision

Numerous research studies indicate that employees are more likely to find meaning at work if their job helps them achieve some longer-term goals. Typically, this involves a leader understanding the far-reaching goals an employee wants to achieve and helping them see how their work is contributing to that.

And it's not about linking to the organisational vision alone. In his study, *'I'm not mopping the floors, I'm putting a man on the moon': How NASA leaders enhanced the meaningfulness of work by changing the meaning of work*', Andrew Carton unearthed the paradoxical finding that leaders' efforts to articulate organisational aspirations can sometimes actually undermine employees' ability to see the connections.

He studied hundreds of documents written by John F Kennedy to uncover how he galvanised NASA employees to all work together to get a man to the moon. There were two main insights. The first one is the importance of articulating a common goal, not just to harness the collective energy but also to help people build a connection between their work and the organisation's highest aims. The second was helping people see a connection between their work and that vision through using subgoals. Subgoals help people monitor their progress towards the main goal.

This requires reconstructing day-to-day work to the organisation's objective, helping employees understand how a series of low level tasks are related to say, the bigger picture of putting a man on the moon.

Typically, I find in most high-growth organisations that the CEO has an inspiring mission such as 'To reach 1 million customers by 2025'. This may generate a lot of excitement, but there is often confusion as to how that is going to happen. For those who are already working hard, that might seem to be quite an overwhelming goal when they are already overworked.

Carton found that leaders must spend time building a blueprint that enables employees to connect the overall aim of the organisation to more concrete day-to-day work activities rather than focusing on an abstract organisational ideal that carries less meaning. This requires spending time with each of your employees during one-on-ones and working out their individual subgoals to achieving the company vision. Ask questions such as, 'What are three goals you would like to achieve this quarter that are connected to the company vision?'

It's also important that you are clear on the importance of each of your direct report's jobs. In his book *Good Authority*, Jonathan Raymond found that leaders need to consider, 'What roles are in my team? Why do they matter?' Deeply understanding each job role ensures that you are better able to connect that to your employees. Even better is if you ask them, 'Hey Katrina, I'm trying to work out why your role exists. This is why I think it matters. But why do you think it exists?'

STRATEGY 1: LINKING PERSONAL IMPACT

This helps provide important context for people to make better decisions and prioritise their tasks more effectively.

Identify meaningful progress

Imagine you had to walk 20 kilometres (12.5 miles) in one day. Which of the following would you find more motivating?

Being told:

A. How far you are expected to go and being kept informed of progress along the way.

B. 'This is the long march you hear about doing,' with no information about the total distance or how far you have travelled.

C. To march 15 kilometres, then when you reach the 14-kilometre mark you are told you still have six kilometres left to go.

D. To march 25 kilometres, then when you reach 14 kilometres you are told you only have six more left to march.

A 1982 study by D Eden and A Shani measured the importance of feedback through researching US soldiers during intensive training. Four groups each received one of the instructions above. Group A, who knew exactly how they were progressing, had the best performance and least stress. Group C who thought they were marching only fifteen kilometres but were told they had a further six kilometres to go performed next best. Group D, who were given good news at the 14-kilometre mark, rated third best. While Group B, who received no information about how far they were going or their progress, performed worst.

We need regular feedback to inform us how we are tracking to motivate us to stay the course. Many of us need to feel that we are making progress and that our work is contributing to something important.

Measurement and feedback provide an important sense of momentum which is, critical to increasing performance and motivation. They reinforce we are doing the right things or show us when we need to change our approach. When we don't receive feedback, or receive it after an activity is performed, it negatively impacts our self-confidence and sense of achievement.

Yet, so many well-meaning leaders avoid giving feedback, either because they are uncomfortable raising negative information or they don't realise the importance of providing progress updates.

That's why annual performance reviews are so derided within organisations. Providing feedback at an annual performance review isn't enough. The infrequency of feedback means that employees are missing out on regular learning opportunities.

As previously mentioned, running effective one-on-one meetings is a powerful performance development tool because faster feedback loops accelerate progress towards goals. Here are some tips for these:

- Co-create a one-on-one agenda with your direct report so that you know how they want to receive feedback. This ensures you avoid making people feel stuck or wounded.
- Look at how they want their progress to be measured. At work, a lot of measurements can be meaningless for individuals. Help your employees measure what matters to them. Work with them to uncover what makes them feel successful at the end of the day or week. For example, if they are writing code, it could be the number of errors they have fixed or the number of attempts to improve code.

STRATEGY 1: LINKING PERSONAL IMPACT

In addition to providing feedback in one-on-ones, you can also make yourself available during the day such as a scheduled 30-minute block in your calendar for employees to drop in.

> *Making feedback a daily occurrence encourages people to challenge, share and learn. It becomes part of how the organisation (and team) operates. It will also make it easier for employees to challenge the leader, which is a key component of psychological safety.*

Often in an organisation there can be projects that have some pretty long, arduous timelines. Sometimes the end goal shifts, while other times, the task is long and tortuous. Not only that, for some jobs there is no job security in the role (such as scientists who need grants to keep going). In these instances where employees may feel like they aren't making progress, it's beneficial to ensure they can see that they are learning important career-building skills, or that the change in direction will make a better end-user product.

Visual dashboards are also powerful reminders of how progress is being made, as are weekly business updates by management. Furthermore, sharing progress updates with team members in team meetings is important, as well as asking, 'What have you learnt this week?' during one-on-ones. This helps people to connect that their time and effort hasn't been wasted. It ensures people don't lose sight of the finishing line, so that they continue to be inspired and motivated to keep going.

Connecting to end users is very important for our intrinsic motivation levels. We'll take a look into this topic in the next chapter.

Reflection

- Are you creating stretch goals for yourself? How can you model the importance of challenging yourself to your team members? How can you support people more in achieving their goals?

- Have you spent time reflecting on the importance of each of your direct report's jobs, in terms of how their role contributes to the organisation, your team and to you?

- How can you more regularly include progress updates in your team meetings (including your own personal goals)?

- Purpose is all about evoking an emotional response. How can you help people feel their purpose? It's not about telling people their purpose, it's about helping them feel it in action through calling it out and amplifying its impact.

Implementation

- Work with each employee to create their own goals that are tied to the team's overarching goal (and encourage each team member to share their goals at team meetings). Then, work with them to measure their progress.

Strategy 2:
Understanding Beneficiaries

In the previous section, we discussed how important it is to help your direct reports connect how their individual effort contributes to the broader goal of the organisation. This provides contextual understanding of the intrinsic impact of their work. It's also really important to also connect how others benefit from their work. This will help improve motivation, job satisfaction and productivity – the extrinsic impact.

Essentially, people love their job if it matters whether they show up to work. Most of us have had the experience of turning up to work sick, not because we wanted to, but because we knew that we were needed. Our presence and effort made a real difference to the people around us.

Helping employees link to how their work matters is crucial for improving motivation levels. Motivation comes from within. It's not external, so a leader can't actually motivate people. You can't go up to an employee and say, 'You need to be more motivated.' Rather what you can do is create an environment in which motivated people can flourish.

Everyone wants to feel that they have played a part in shaping the world around them. Contribution is a powerful driver fuelling our highest personal ambitions. It ensures that we support those around us.

According to research by Francesca Gino, a behavioural scientist at Harvard Business School, there are both psychological and performance benefits to connecting employees to the beneficiaries of their work. In particular, interactions with the beneficiaries of one's work can be highly motivating because they heighten workers' perception of the impact of their tasks.

Let's take a look at how to connect to three different type of beneficiaries.

Connect your team with the internal customer

In organisations, there is usually an outward focus on external customers because they bring in revenue. Often, I find that departments such as finance, HR and facilities management that serve internal customers get forgotten about. It creates a lot of tension between internal support functions and their revenue-generating peers. The quest for serving external customers is often seen as most important. Yet, while this singular focus is critical, as an organisation gets bigger it can be detrimental for getting working done within an organisation.

The solution is for every department to grasp the importance of both internal and external customers with everyone focused on how to best serve the paying customer. Underlying this is the need to help everyone in an organisation understand the work of each department.

An interesting field study by Paul Green at the University of Texas at a tomato-processing company in California asked a group of employees who were harvesting tomatoes to watch a short video from a colleague within a different team talking about the positive impact the work of that harvesting team had on them in the factory. The control

STRATEGY 2: UNDERSTANDING BENEFICIARIES

group didn't watch the video. A few weeks after this, the productivity of the employees who watched the video had improved by 7%. This was measured by the tonnes of tomatoes harvested per hour compared to those in the control group.

Where possible, encourage team members to spend time with internal customers. The goal is for your team to understand the goals, language and priorities of other teams, so they can better understand how their work affects them. When employees discover how their work positively impacts others it becomes highly motivating. This also strengthens people's sense of belongingness and connection.

One organisation that does this well is Adore Beauty, an Australian online beauty retailer. In 2000, Kate Morris and James Height co-founded the company from their garage in Melbourne. Through trials and tribulations they built their company into the behemoth that is now on the Australian stock exchange.

Back in 2016, I met Kate through a CEO roundtable I hosted for fast growing companies. Not long after, I caught up with her, as she was struggling with growth and the usual leadership teams issues that plague a start-up founder. Three years later when we caught up again, she had turned things around and grown the company from 25 to 145 employees. In 2020, Adore Beauty had a successful IPO.

One of the biggest issues she faced during growth was having staff on multiple sites. She shared her strategies with me, 'Now, that we are split across multiple locations it's hard for people to know everyone. Before, people in marketing could speak to people in the warehouse if they had questions because they would know someone. Now, they don't. As we have gotten bigger, we have had to work really hard to encourage teams to physically meet or have video calls.

'As part of our induction process, even if people are working in the office, they spend a day at the factory doing pick and pack, just to meet people there and understand how everything works end-to-end. I find that when people don't understand what another department does that's when they get annoyed with them. They would say, 'Why didn't they do this?' Now, marketing is aware of what is involved with warehousing putting a new product on the shelf at three pm on Monday because they know first-hand that's their busiest day in the warehouse.

To further help teams understand one another at a deeper level, Morris found that getting teams to work together cross-functionally also improved contextual understanding. She said, 'It's been a useful thing to get other teams to work together at an offsite with brand and marketing teams sharing their KPIs so everyone understands what they are trying to perform to. So they realised that if they feature a product in marketing communication and the other brand team member is being measured on how many out-of-stocks they have, that, if they don't give them a chance to order extra, then they will be out-of-stock and their performance will look bad. Or perhaps it's a low margin product and the brand's team's KPI is how much gross margin they deliver to the business. So again, it might make their performance look bad, so then they could ask for their help and ask them, "I was thinking about you, does this work or would this be better?"'

In addition to getting teams together to better understand how their results are measured and how work gets done, Morris found that bringing cross-functional team leaders together regularly helped reduce silos and build trust. Morris added, 'Get different cross-functional managers to meet twice a month and talk about what they are doing in their department so that fulfilment knows what production is doing. This team meeting is with the whole operations group and each function talks through their metrics. What's increasing/decreasing? What do our costs look like? Then, they go around and get each functional head to talk about their initiatives related to broader strategy and where they are with that, as well as any new initiatives they wish to bring to the table.'

Key to making these cross-functional team meetings work is a relaxed atmosphere where people openly share their progress, roadblocks and concerns in the spirit of helping one another achieve. This is very much in keeping with a mastermind group that fosters accountability, as people don't want to let one another down. Morris found that, 'Getting together cross functionally brings forth a lot of good things that you normally don't get if meeting to discuss the one area.'

Connect your team with the external customer

Ultimately, organisations have to solve customer problems to stay in business. The reality is you can't make good customer decisions if you are siloed. Yet, the customer can often get forgotten about as an organisation becomes larger. It is important to help your people understand how their work benefits customers.

The best method to do that is for employees to hear firsthand from customers how the organisation's product or service improves their life.

In a field study from Adam Grant of the Wharton School, fundraisers who were attempting to secure scholarship donations felt more motivated when they had contact with scholarship recipients. Instead of feeling like their job involved monotonous phone calls they became absorbed in helping to fund tuition. In fact, one group doubled in weekly time on phone and tripled in revenue.

It's important to help your employees think about who would be worse off if they didn't do their job. Reframing *for who your work matters* can be a powerful motivator to improve our results.

Share letters from customers, create customer video testimonials, encourage non-customer facing staff to attend client meetings or send your employees to work at a customer premises. These ideas can be highly motivational, and also ensure alignment to customer requirements. Furthermore, it sends an important message to customers that their business is truly valued.

Connect your team to how their role helps you

Another important benefit to communicate is to illuminate your direct reports on how their work helps you.

Let's face it: some of the work direct reports undertake might seem a little bit meaningless and tedious. Yet, it is work that saves you a lot of time and of course, sanity, which frees you up to work on high priority tasks that advance the organisation forward.

In the movie *The Devil Wears Prada*, Andy (Ann Hathaway) is the junior assistant to the editor-in-chief of *Runway* magazine, Miranda (Meryl Streep). The role is demeaning, demanding and poor-paying. Andy works hard to please her boss who expects her to work overtime and complete almost impossible tasks. It's not surprising that Miranda has trouble keeping assistants due to her constant demands in a high pressure industry. Andy toughs it out because she dreams of being a writer and hopes the job will provide her with a good reference. While a good reference can motivate us to stick around in a thankless job, our work is more meaningful when we can connect to how we are of service to others. In the movie, Miranda never explains to Andy how her contribution makes her life easier. Instead, she demands professional excellence even though she provides little context, support or training. Given that the job was in the fashion industry, it might have helped her keep assistants for a little bit longer (a 2013 Adam Grant study found fashion design jobs are considered the most meaningless).

For any job role that involves mindless tasks, help people see the meaning in it through reframing the work as an important act of service. Identify how their effort helps you, whether that's reducing the stress of preparing for an important presentation or ensuring you can submit your monthly reports on time. Acknowledging that a task is tedious, but helpful to you, is also important.

Best practice to bring more compassion to your leadership style

Your direct reports are eager for your approval as you hold the power to their job security. They are always watching you to make sure that you are pleased with their work and that their job is safe. They need to be reassured that you are there for them and that you have got their back.

At the heart of it, employees want to know that you care about them. They want to know that you see them as being more than just a tool of productivity. When you seem disconnected or distant from team members, they won't be sure where you stand on things or how to approach you.

The best leaders bring out the best in people. The most productive and profitable companies have a leadership style where leaders spend time developing and recognising their staff, being open to feedback (including negative comments) and promoting teamwork.

Strengthening the bonds between yourself and your direct reports is critical to their job satisfaction, as well as your own. Developing and maintaining healthy working relationships with employees motivates stronger commitment and better performance. One-on-ones are an important tool to do this, but how we interact is also critical.

When improving any leadership capability, it is important to work on improving your self-awareness or emotional intelligence (EQ). People with empathy are good at recognising the feelings of others, even when those feelings may not be obvious. As a result, empathetic people are usually excellent at managing relationships.

Here are seven practices to bring more compassion to your leadership style, while raising your emotional intelligence at the same time.

1. Show interest in understanding people

One of the most important steps in building trust and connection in your team is to spend time understanding each individual. We don't trust people who are only interested in themselves. Taking the time to understand people is key to improving trust in relationships. This involves avoiding talking about yourself and hijacking the conversation so that it's all about you. It requires putting aside self-interested and protectionist tendencies and accepting people for who they are, not who you want them to be.

High trust leaders know how to make others feel important. They understand that not everyone is the same and customise their interactions to suit the individual. They ask incisive questions to uncover communication, work styles and preferences for receiving feedback. They seek to further understand people's aspirations, strengths, weakness and emotional triggers.

This information is important as it enables you to know what drives each individual so you can better motivate and push people forward. Learning about each of your direct reports helps you align each individual's self-interest with the collective interest of the group.

Luckily, this process has been made easier by online assessments that you can get your team members to undertake. There are a variety of them around such as DISC or Drake's P3. Assessments can take the guess work out of how people like to work and communicate, making them a powerful discussion tool that not only improves self-awareness, but also provides clarity for others.

An effective approach to building stronger relationships involves being curious. Leading through asking questions helps us better customise our approach with others in a way that suits them.

Typically, any type of disagreement that we have with others stems from a lack of understanding of a person's individuality, preferences or point of view. When we invest the time to understand another person, it is like respecting and honouring their soul. The process implicitly sends people a message that they are important and valued. Like the Indian greeting 'Namaste': the God within me acknowledges the God within you.

2. Listen, listen and listen again

Great leaders know that really important information surfaces when they keep quiet. It is when transformation occurs, not only in meetings, which we looked at earlier, but in any work context.

A highly empathetic leader does not dominate a workplace conversation, rather they let people talk things through. Really listening to employees shows that you are present and focused. It demonstrates that you care more than any words can alone.

Some of the tricks that I learnt when I was a market researcher undertaking in-depth face-to-face interviews was to ask a tricky question and then look down at my paper. People dislike silence and are more likely to fill the space and start talking, even when they aren't sure what to say. Asking, 'Is there anything else?' or 'Is there anything else I haven't raised?' also helps to elicit further information.

When talking to staff members, use good quality, open-ended questions that are outcome based. Questions that focus on results include 'what' or 'how' questions. Another great option is 'what if' or 'have you ever' questions. They encourage people to think differently and gives them permission to be playful.

Avoid asking too many close-ended questions that require a yes or no response. They aren't very revealing and can stop the conversation pretty quickly.

Some examples of good quality questions include:

- What was your thinking on that?
- What would you do if you were in my role?
- How do you feel about what I'm saying?
- What if you did it this way?
- What did you learn from customers this week?

3. Believe in your people

Belief is critical to getting results in life. It's the foundational platform for success, as it effectively drives our behaviours and actions.

One of the features of a high trust leader is that they obtain the best out of their people because they believe in them. They see and expect the best.

STRATEGY 2: UNDERSTANDING BENEFICIARIES

The good news is that when we believe in our people, they believe in us. Known as The Pygmalion Effect, it is a type of self-fulfilling prophecy that when a manager expects more of their subordinates it leads them to greater achievement.

When we believe in others it provides them with the support structure to strive and keep going when they make mistakes. People are more likely to rise to the occasion when they know people believe in them.

Believing in people also ties in to having high expectations of them. It powerfully reframes how people see themselves in a more positive and beneficial way. After all, we live up to-or down to other people's expectations of us.

> *Fostering the confidence to do well is critical. Without confidence, people lack the conviction to take on tough challenges, which manifests in helplessness and powerlessness.*

Belief is important on three different levels – for individuals, teams and the organisation itself. It means communicating that you believe:

- in the company vision, product offerings and positive impact in the world,
- that the team has the collective intelligence to overcome any challenges and create a beneficial outcome for the client,
- that each individual has the ability to improve their skills and capabilities.

During change, expressing that you believe that your team will surmount the current challenges is critical to helping people through tough times.

> **Reflection**
>
> - Do you believe that your team will get through a difficult patch? What about yourself? What can you say to let people know that you believe in them?

4. Assume Positive Intent

Thanks to bad experiences, a cynical society or even the way we were brought up, we tend to search for people's faults. Without being aware of it, we act like surly teenagers automatically finding the negative in anyone and anything.

In the book, *The Power of Bad: How the Negativity Effect Rules Us and How We Can Rule It*, authors Roy F Baumeister and John Tierney argue that there is a 'universal tendency for negative events and emotions to affect us more strongly than positive ones.' We 'see the hostile face in the crowd' but 'miss all the friendly smiles'.

Our built-in negativity bias stops us from seeing the good in people we work with and focusses on the bad. For many of us, we do this subconsciously. We critique newcomers with whatever we value – whether it's their looks, sense of style, how they speak, level of education, intelligence or where they live.

I am embarrassed to admit that I judge people on how they look. Growing up in a family where physical appearances mattered, I absorbed that belief. Strangely enough, it was my teenage daughter who took me to task. One Saturday morning, watching *Rage* (a music video show that I've watched every week since it started), I made a negative remark about a singer and how they looked. My daughter was annoyed and told me why my comment was inappropriate. She was right (and made me so pleased that Generation Z is better at this than Gen X). I

STRATEGY 2: UNDERSTANDING BENEFICIARIES

now consciously avoid allowing these quite petty beliefs to impact my initial thoughts on people. And if I say them out loud, the good news is I quickly get correctly with an exasperated, 'Mother!' (which is her term for me when I misbehave).

But it's not just our deeply ingrained beliefs that impact what we think of others. It's also past experiences. All of us will encounter people that take advantage of us and treat us disrespectfully. These experiences tend to make us fearful of others and expect the worst. If we let them, they can irrevocably impact our interactions with others.

Low trust leaders tend to have a more negative disposition to the world around them and expect the worst in everyone and everything. They lock up needed supplies, create senseless rules and hold back from sharing important information. Their modus operandi is that 'trust must be earned.' They perceive people as distrustful not realising that they are often inadvertently causing trust issues.

Unfortunately, when we leverage the mighty power of confirmation bias, we get what we expect.

Confirmation bias is the tendency to interpret new evidence as confirmation of one's existing beliefs or theories. In business, it means employees see what they want to see and hear what they want to hear to support their beliefs. It can result in business forecasts or plans being unrealistic or projects that aren't viable being resourced. Leaders ignore market data, customer or employee feedback if it doesn't match their beliefs. It's a cognitive bias that results in poor problem solving, policies and planning. But what it is not commonly talked about is that it also decreases our ability to form strong relationships in the workplace with people who are different to us or who may have changed. If you think people can't be trusted, they will most likely act in ways you perceive untrustworthy, mirroring your subconscious behaviours.

So how do you take advantage of this to help move your team firmly into the achievement zone? Through swapping over the negative filter from which we unintentionally view the world to a positive, rosy-coloured hue.

Confirmation bias can be positive if we use it to believe in the good of the people around us.

This is critical for leading employees who are working from home because it's more difficult to read non-verbal cues, which can lead to misunderstandings. It requires not jumping to conclusions when something has gone wrong in a project and realising that sometimes things are outside the control of employees.

Think about the last time you responded to bad news. Did you jump to conclusions, blame others or complain? Or do you calmly ask for more information?

Taking the time to source as much information as you can before making a judgement ensures focusing on a high quality solution. Resorting to finger-pointing, second-guessing or blaming others can be incredibly damaging to relationships.

Think of the expression 'slow to anger, quick to love'. Operating with that perspective reduces the risk of bringing chaos and animosity to a situation. It avoids automatically thinking that a person is 'lazy', 'stupid' or 'disorganised'.

Managers who operate with positive assumptions, encourage employees to respond in kind. It means that an unpopular or questionable management action is accepted because employees trust that there is more to the story.

STRATEGY 2: UNDERSTANDING BENEFICIARIES

> *When everyone leads with thinking the best, it provides comfort during times of rapid change and growth.*

One caveat that I would like to point out is that we have to be realistic with our rose-tinted glasses. There are times when people are at fault and if there are complaints about their behaviours then this does need to be investigated. Toxic behaviours can run rampant when we refuse to believe our employees are negligent or behaving poorly and we don't hold them accountable.

5. Be vulnerable

A common statement made about trust is that you need vulnerability. At its core, this requires leaders to be humble. Having humility is when you let people know that you don't have all the answers and that you make mistakes. It sends a powerful signal of togetherness that models both vulnerability and humility.

One way to think of vulnerability is like a dog that greets a stranger by showing their belly. It's instantly disarming. But revealing our soft underbelly can be extremely daunting for anyone, let alone a leader. On the other hand, humility is more about a dog admitting that they chewed their owner's socks.

According to research by Daniel Coyle, author of *The Culture Code*, the big moments in a leader's career aren't during an inspirational speech or the successful launch of a big strategy. Instead, they are based on the little moments of confession, when leaders admit to a mistake or a weakness.

This goes outside the norm of how we expect a leader to behave. It's been a common management assumption for centuries that leaders have to know all the answers. Employees cling to the belief that their boss is all knowing and leaders do their best to perpetuate that myth. But it creates issues for both leaders and employees. For leaders it makes them act with hubris and defensiveness when they are questioned; for employees it tends to reduce their ability to think for themselves and makes them more likely to think negatively of their leaders when they don't meet expectations.

Admitting mistakes sends a powerful signal that you're accountable and human. This small act sends a powerful message to others that it's okay to make the wrong decision. Leading by example creates a safe space where people feel confident enough to share their own fallibilities.

Researchers Karina Schumann and Carol S Dweck studied the correlation between theories of personality and the willingness to accept responsibility for a transgression. They compared people with a fixed mindset with those with a growth mindset to uncover if there was a difference to admitting fault.

Fixed mindset individuals believe that their basic qualities such as intelligence and talent are fixed. They avoid putting themselves into situations where they might fail. While those with a growth mindset believe they can always develop their abilities further. They see failure as a confirmation of their immutable abilities and an opportunity to learn and grow from the experience.

Schumann and Dweck discovered that people with a growth mindset are more likely to admit wrongdoing because they tend to view the situation as an opportunity for them to grow as a person. Rather than feel threatened like those with a fixed mindset.

STRATEGY 2: UNDERSTANDING BENEFICIARIES

A leader who refuses to admit mistakes keeps their team firmly in the abatement, anxiety and apathy zones where people are afraid to fail.

> **Talking about errors encourages a cycle of learning, experimenting and improving that creates a culture of innovation and creativity. It's how you get teams into the achievement zone.**

Not being honest about your weaknesses also creates distrust with those around you. People will subconsciously not trust a leader who does not admit fault. Such behaviour subtly lets people know that truth and transparency aren't important. It implicitly tells team members to lie or hide any mistakes that they make. A strong team culture occurs when people feel safe enough to discuss uncomfortable truths. And it happens in small moments when a leader humbly reveals their own weaknesses. This moment of truth is called a vulnerability loop that transfers trust to other people in the room, just like a virus.

The vulnerability loop stems from research undertaken by Dr Jeff Polzer, from Harvard Business School. He undertook a study where complete strangers had to ask questions of one another. Group A participants were asked standard personal information sharing questions such as, 'What was the best gift you received and why?' While Group B participants received uncomfortable questions such as, 'Is there something that you've dreamed of doing for a long time? Why haven't you done it?'

Group A participants asked questions that allowed them to stay in their comfort zone, in other words, the standard types of questions we ask people at work functions. Group B questions were awkward and generated confession. They also melted the ice between strangers. But it did something else that was extremely powerful. It created vulnerability, allowing Group B strangers to feel 24% closer versus those in Group A. In fact, one Group B pair ended up getting married.

But this is where it gets really interesting.

We often assume that being vulnerable is going to make us feel ashamed in some way. That we are going to expose ourselves (and our fluffy, cute bellies) and people will see us for who we really are and make fun of us (just like that common dream we experience of walking down the street naked). Yet, the benefits of being able to be vulnerable in a workplace are huge. When leaders admit to having weaknesses and ask for help, it sets the behavioural tone for others, enabling team member to brush aside their insecurities, trust one another and get to work. In fact, if there is no vulnerable moment, people will default to covering up their weaknesses resulting in dysfunctional interactions and work quality.

But here's the catch. Dr Polzer's research found that vulnerability isn't about the sender. It's all about the receiver.

And this is what we often get wrong. A common complaint by employees is that their leaders need to be more vulnerable. And yes, leaders do need to be humble and ask for help, in order to build trust. But few people ever look at themselves and consider whether they are enabling those around them to be vulnerable.

If the second person pretends they don't have any flaws or ignores the sender's vulnerable comment, it creates distrust in the team impacting team dynamics (especially if the leader ignores the signal). In fact, Polzer has become skilled at observing the moment of truth when the vulnerability signal travels through the group. He says, 'You can actually see people relax and connect and start to trust.'

How we react to other people disclosing personal information is critical. Not just by leaders to their people, but vice versa. If we aren't taught how to empower those around us to share insights and fears, we are contributing to reducing psychologically safety. The outcome is that people will fear taking risks in the group and will shut down further contribution and commitment.

The good news is that if the thought of being vulnerable to your teammates makes you feel uncomfortable, just remember, it's not about you. Your being vulnerable unlocks empathy in others. How they handle that is critical to team dynamics.

Vulnerability is so much more than just disclosing our own personal frailties. It's about how we support others in their vulnerability.

Reflection

- When was the last time you admitted you were wrong to your team members? If you can't remember, what small step can you take to admit a mistake or you don't know something?
- How do you respond when someone admits mistakes or reveals a weakness? Do you thank them for sharing and congratulate them on talking about difficult stuff?
- How do you encourage your direct reports and peers to give you feedback on your performance?

6. Avoid Affinity

Early in my career, I was interviewed by the founder and CEO of a market research firm and two of his directors. The interview was going well, but it went to a whole new level when there was a question raised about the school I went to on my CV.

Luckily for me, I had attended a prestigious Melbourne girl's school. One of the super star 27-year-old directors had also attended the same school (a year above me). The CEO who was clearly in awe of her immediately felt more comfortable with me. In all of their minds, I was a good fit.

Unfortunately, I wasn't. I was quite different to the gung-ho and low empathy directors. They regularly reprimanded me for not being more assertive like them. Well, they called it being assertive; I saw it more as being aggressive and pushy. Working there was a struggle as I had no support of the people around me. I was shunned and put into a small, dark office. It felt like they were always disappointed that I wasn't the personality type they expected, while I was always uncomfortable because they were constantly telling me to be like them when I couldn't see any qualities that I admired.

A common technique in building trust in the workplace is that people look for points of commonality. It might be growing up in the same suburb, barracking for the same football team or attending the same university. While it does work in bringing some people together, the risk is that it alienates and excludes other, who are different.

Interestingly, Adam Grant refers to a study that similarities are more likely to build trust when they are rare. In an experiment when people discovered they shared type E fingerprints they felt a little close. But when they were told the different type was rare (2%) they felt a closer bond and were significantly likely to help each other.

If you want to build trust, avoid trying to only find commonalities. Look for uncommon commonalities. In a workplace, we want to fit in and stand out. But when we have too many people that fit in, it creates a less cognitive diverse workplace creating groupthink.

STRATEGY 2: UNDERSTANDING BENEFICIARIES

Not only that, the problem with building trust just through affinity is that it occurs through standard personal information sharing questions, in other words, conversations that are fairly superficial. What we really need to be doing is being more inquisitive and interested in others, asking Group B questions – the ones that are uncomfortable and generate confession.

7. Watch your reactions

How we react to bad news or things people do that displease us can work against us building trust with others. It's a really important non-verbal cue that sometimes sends mixed messages.

I have a smile that doesn't look like a smile. It's more of a grimace. I have to purposefully smile, to let people know that I am okay with a situation when things get tough. My thinking face looks more like a grumpy face.

Even my husband, who knows me better than anyone, will read my facial expression and say 'You're angry with me,' and I have to assure him I'm just processing. Honestly, sometimes I get so shocked by bad news that I barely have time to register my facial expression. Having said that, I do have a face that is more like an overly expressive Muppet. I walk down the street and let my facial expressions run wild. Playing poker is not a good use of my time.

So when I'm given bad news, I have to watch my reactions. I grew up in a volatile family where any bad news was taken as the end of the world with lots of moaning, overly expressive sighing and long rants about the unfairness of the world. That is my default reaction spiced up with the type of language only a sailor would feel comfortable with. And while swearing has been found to allow you to handle suffering better, reducing stress and alleviating pain, it doesn't look good in front of people. Particularly, when you have impressionable children and a husband who detests swearing. I am also pretty sure I freaked out my team more than necessary in my early leadership days through unbridled swear fests (but oh, did they *feel* good!).

While swearing and over-reacting are obviously things we need to tone down, it's the little non-verbal signals that we send out that cause the most issues. The thing to remember is that our employees are reading our body language, as well as what we say. Our body language conveys a lot of information. Learning how to moderate our responses and facial expressions ensures that people feel that interacting with us is one of reward and not of risk (or high drama, as in my younger days).

After all, no one would want to share errors with us if we react to employee errors by crossing our arms, looking grumpy, refusing to answer questions or swearing. Yet, so many leaders do some of these without even knowing.

Strategy 3: Focusing on People and Parts

A common source of frustration often cited by employees is that they do not understand the organisation's overarching vision and how everything connects together.

A study by researchers at the London Business School and MIT's Sloan School of Management found only a third of senior managers could correctly identify what the CEO had identified as the firm's top three priorities. Yet, the most surprising finding was that when the researchers dug a little deeper, they discovered that this became more of an issue when someone in another department asked for help. A department head would say yes to the request, but would fail to attend to it, mainly because they didn't know how vital it was to the organisation as a whole, so other priorities for their business unit called their attention. The result was senior managers trusted colleagues in other departments or business units to deliver only 10% of the time.

Rebecca Homkes, who worked on the survey said, 'When you drop one or two levels below the CEO, your ability to form a holistic picture is simply lost, in this vacuum you're leaving managers across the organisation to prioritise by themselves.'

As a team leader, you play an important role in ensuring change and alignment occur. Your direct employees trust you because they have a closer relationship to you. They're less likely to trust the CEO or a senior executive who they barely see or who doesn't know their name. You're an important linchpin that builds trust across the organisation. You make the strategy come alive.

Employees require a consistent vision that provides a guiding light to evaluate risks on the fly, spot problems and be more responsive to one another. Your role is to tie your team's work to the company vision, together with a holistic understanding of the interactions between all moving parts in your organisation. This supports employees with the right context to take initiatives and make fast decisions, so that projects are delivered on time and with high quality deliverables.

Without this common or shared understanding a raft of issues occurs, including confusion around accountabilities and priorities, which slows down decision-making. This limits a team's ability to help other teams due to a lack of understanding of where another team fits within the broader landscape.

Let's go through the steps to connect all the parts together in an organisation.

Connect everyone to a clear purpose

One of the common issues leaders face is how to bring employees on board when change is required. Underpinning this requires ensuring employees will continue to trust leadership when things are in a state of flux.

According to Jim Collins, who spent 25 years researching leadership, the foundational element to leading an organisation is guiding by a set of core values and purpose (known together as core ideology).

When organisations face uncertainty, core purpose becomes even more important — not less so. That's because the 'what and how' of

STRATEGY 3: FOCUSING ON PEOPLE AND PARTS

business need to change more frequently in a volatile world. This leaves purpose, the 'why', as the primary compass for navigating key decisions. It's critical information to communicate to employees to get their thinking aligned and to reduce fear. It also sets up the foundations for trust.

One of the most common attributes of companies with high performance workplace cultures is that they have a clear, well-specified purpose that states both how and why the company makes a positive impact on the world. It's their fundamental reason for existence beyond just making money.

This is not a feel-good statement. It actually works towards pulling people forward especially in difficult times (and good). It helps people make better decisions and it generates tremendous energy that aligns everyone towards a common cause.

> *The central pillar for building trust is a corporate purpose that's defined by a genuine commitment to the social good. Purpose is what a company stands for and creates value for employees, customers and society.*

In my work with organisations, I have found a distinct shift since the pandemic. Now, people are looking for more signs of empathy in the workplace with women really driving this emotional requirement.

A social purpose provides employees with the context that demonstrates how much the organisation cares, which in turn makes them less likely to believe the organisation just exists to make money. It makes sense because we're more likely to trust a company if we can see evidence of consistent action and behaviour that indicates good intent.

A meaningful purpose embedded in an organisation connects the motivational differences between creative- and numbers-driven employees. Creatives are not motivated around company success through metrics or profit numbers. They tend to feel icky that a marketing campaign they are putting together is to manipulate people into buying. To offset the ickiness, they require a company purpose that tangibly makes a difference to the world, rather than line the pockets of shareholders. That can be through company donations to worthwhile causes, human rights and environmental initiatives or even the opportunity to volunteer during work hours.

By contrast, numbers-driven employees are motivated by profit and making the numbers. Ticking tasks off a checklist and being part of launching a successful initiative motivates them. The challenge is to ensure that the company purpose unifies the total workforce and provides meaningful in-group status, rather than allowing employees to drift into silos and bond only with those in their department. Without a clear, consistent and cohesive purpose employees drift into silo-based behaviours as they fail to understand how other departments connect to the work that they do.

Companies that focus on everyday functional tasks such as sales targets and KPIs subtly tell their employees that's what is important. Over time people's headspace revolves around making targets but they forget the reason why they are really employed. Essentially, creating efficient, scalable business processes engineers the meaning out of work. While a company can survive for some time on this path, over time they forget about the customer and become complacent. This increases the degree of executional difficulty and increases customer complaints or claims.

STRATEGY 3: FOCUSING ON PEOPLE AND PARTS

That's why it's so important that employees understand the real meaning behind the work that they do, the purpose of the organisation and the impact they are helping create for the world. Otherwise, they become so caught up in the day-to-day that they're unable to notice when customers aren't happy and processes aren't working.

Focusing on purpose rather than profits is what builds business confidence and therefore, trust. It pivots the organisation towards a stakeholder approach that focuses on the needs of different groups when making decisions about employees, customers, local communities, stockholders and debtors, rather than the more traditional approach of considering one type of stakeholder.

In addition to the core purpose, leaders need to espouse and model core values. These are the behaviours that define the culture and are reinforced through your HR systems and leadership communication on a daily basis.

An effective leader helps key people connect their core values and core talents to the organisation, to their customers and their lives.

> *Purpose is always about how we add value to others and it is present when we engage in activities.*

The objective here is to ensure people feel connected to one another through alignment with their purpose and their belief in the organisation's purpose and value. This even includes specifying a clear team purpose.

You can do this by asking people questions about the purpose so they can connect their daily work. Ask questions such as, 'How do you think the work you are doing helps our purpose?' or 'What can you do to help our company accomplish our purpose?'

Strengthen employees by helping them understand how the contextual factors of their jobs play out. Design jobs so people know what's expected of them.

Connect people within your team

As social beings, we love making emotional connections with others and being seen for who we are rather than just as an agent performing a role. A global study of engagement from the ADP Research Institute found that if employees consider themselves part of a team they are twice as likely to feel engaged in their work.

Yet, *Harvard Business Review* published a study undertaken by Oracle and Engage for Success that found that many teams that appear engaged in employee engagement metrics may be less engaged than first thought. Over a three-year period, research was undertaken with 41 work teams spanning nine industry sectors. The study found that one-third of teams fell into a category called pseudo-engaged. These teams appeared engaged both in surveys and in the eyes of management. Yet, on closer inspection exhibited some troubling signs of disengagement, such as antipathy toward colleagues and dishonesty to managers.

The gap in perceived and actual engagement levels was that these teams were made up of people who tended to be ambitious and highly engaged at an individual level, but not so engaged at the teamwork level. The truth was that they really weren't that invested in their teams.

The study looked into teams at a hospital ward. One highly engaged team was motivated by a strong sense of purpose and commitment to high quality patient care. But this compassion didn't extend to their own colleagues. Team-based duties tended to be put on the

STRATEGY 3: FOCUSING ON PEOPLE AND PARTS

low priority list. Nurses were reluctant to partner with each other to help prepare the ward for mealtimes or change a patient's bed linen.

Management had been oblivious to these problems because they focused on the teams' successful engagement numbers, which skipped the important measure of teamwork.

When people are measured on their individual performance, they will play the system, deliberately pursuing personal gain at the expense of the team. They place a priority on relationships with those who are in positions of power, stretch their workloads to fill the time or cherry-pick their tasks. These types of behaviours become contagious and before long new starters devalue collaboration as the system rewards individualistic behaviours.

This is very common behaviour for teams in the anxiety and apathy zones. And it's something you always have to work on.

> *Your role as a leader is to continually reinforce how group success revolves around individuals working together for the greater good of customers.*

One important technique to avoid competitive ego-based behaviours overruling a team is through talking about the benefits of collaboration.

A study by a team of Stanford researchers found that even the mere perception of working collectively on a task can supercharge performance. 'Working with others affords enormous social and personal benefits,' the researchers declared. 'Our research found that social cues that conveyed simply that other people treat you as though you are working together on a task – rather than that you are just working on the same task but separately – can have striking effects on motivation.'

Five separate experiments were undertaken where none of the participants actually worked together but were told that they were. Each experiment started with each participant working on a task in isolation. Then, after being introduced to each other as a group, a segment of the group was then primed to think collectively by being told they would work on the task together. This would involve either sharing (or receiving) tips on how to complete the task by a colleague. All groups resulted in an increase in intrinsic motivation.

The remainder of the team were primed to think in solitary terms, with no mention of collaboration whatsoever in their challenge. They would also receive a tip, but rather than receiving it from a colleague, they would receive it from the researcher. In other words, an external party that was not jointly engaged in the task with them. The actual tip itself was identical to both groups.

Participants in the research who were primed to act collaboratively stuck at their task 64% longer than their solitary peers, whilst also reporting higher engagement levels, lower fatigue levels and a higher success rate. Several weeks later they were still engaged in more tasks of a similar nature.

The researchers concluded, 'Our research shows that it is possible to create a spirit of teamwork as people take on challenging individual tasks – a feeling that we're all in this together, working on problems and tasks – and that this sense of working together can inspire motivation.'

> **Telling your direct reports that they are collaborating (even when they aren't) makes them more likely to actually collaborate.**

STRATEGY 3: FOCUSING ON PEOPLE AND PARTS

As the team leader, it is critical that you encourage teams to work collaboratively and understand the importance of being in a team. This can be as simple as stating in team meetings, 'I need you all to work collaboratively on this project' or 'It was so good to see you all collaborating on this task together.'

The findings were similar to other research undertaken in a joint study by the Institute for Corporate Productivity (i4cp) and Rob Cross at Babson College. It found that companies that promoted collaborative working were five times as likely to be high performing.

In the study, with over 1100 companies, only a relative few managed to achieve good results, despite many claiming they had open and collaborative cultures.

So what was the difference?

High achievement collaborative cultures were geared towards enabling collaboration. In a workplace, there are a number of systemic factors that influence how we behave at work. These factors include:

- how information flows throughout the organisation,
- how decisions are made,
- the physical design of workspaces,
- how employee behaviours are measured and rewarded.

You can improve collaboration by recognising and rewarding employees for being collaborative. Uncover the barriers towards collaboration and remove them. Typically, there are hidden incentives that reward individual achievement, rather than group accomplishment.

Never assume teamwork will occur on its own. You need to actively promote and reward the benefits and value of shared responsibilities and outcomes, mutual support and information exchange.

You will know that bonds of trust are being formed when team members feel able to ring each other up to ask questions and share best practices. Moving firmly into the achievement team zone means each team member feels that they are part of the team. The outcome is that people feel motivated to take on big challenges and not let anyone down.

> **Reflection**
>
> - What can you say to your direct reports to prime them to work collaboratively?

Focus on horizontal connectivity

Building strong bonds of connection to our direct reports is critical for performance. Improving shared consciousness requires constructing a strong lattice of trusting relationships across an organisation. Otherwise, silos begin to form with power struggles that can delay product launches or create product recalls.

Previously, I mentioned how important it is for your team to work with other teams and get to know them. But there are times when we there are limited opportunities for people to work with one another across the business. This doesn't mean people shouldn't learn and know about one another.

Successful high trust leaders stand out because they actively build a network of peers and other professionals.

Today, business requires a level of collaboration that's impossible where leaders are self-interested and compete with others. Knowledge work requires bringing together those with the right skills to solve challenges.

STRATEGY 3: FOCUSING ON PEOPLE AND PARTS

Creating a high trust team culture boils down to every employee knowing they can rely on every person around them. It means everyone is committed to performing at a high level and helping their peers achieve as well.

Ensuring that your team stays in the achievement zone requires connecting people together – in their own team and across teams.

One of the common issues with organisations as they get bigger is that departments splinter into their own fiefdoms. Department leaders compete against each other on who has the most people, sales and resources, resulting in an 'us versus them' mentality. Over time, trust is destroyed due to the complexity of misaligned interests slowing execution and growth.

One of the biggest issues I see with building trust in an organisation is that leaders are promoted to leadership positions, but are territorial about their function. They only care about their area of expertise. This is detrimental to leadership team performance who need to act from an enterprise-wide view, rather than an individual perspective.

If you are new to being a leader or you are an established executive, it's important for your career success to think wider rather than getting bogged down into your area of operation. A CEO of a midsize real estate company explained to me, 'It's a funny one. You don't want to be critical of your executives because they say, "This is what I do and I do it well." But they don't understand that's going to be their lot. People go around them because they are too focused on what they are doing. They don't have a wider picture. You have to work out whether it's worth spending the time investing in their leadership development. Sometimes it's better to spend it on those that have the greatest potential.'

Learning to build relationships outside of your technical domain is critical. In today's interconnected world, work is highly interdependent and leaders must work together with different people from diverse backgrounds, skills and experiences.

In workplaces, we continue this separation of job roles, so that other functions appear foreign and unusual. I'll never forget a CEO (with a finance background) who attended one my roundtables claiming that all marketing people wear funny clothes.

These limiting beliefs stop us from making friends with people who do jobs we find boring, unappealing or even beneath us. We don't take the time to find out what they do, why it matters and how they fit in to broader capabilities of the organisation. It is detrimental to leadership team performance that flows on to overall organisational performance.

How leaders interact with others is a subset of their desire to build relationships and understand others. In research I do within organisations, teams will often complain that other teams do not care about their priorities or understand their perspective. The reason could be blamed on hectic work schedules, but usually it is not considered a priority by leaders who just aren't that interested in other people.

The result is that they don't understand why their peers behave in a particular way or don't communicate in the same way as they do. One of the main reasons is that they tend to make assumptions about each other based on their own worldview, failing to take into account the other person's perspective. The result is that they will often get frustrated with each other – butting heads or avoiding each other fearing conflict. This trickles down to the teams under their influence who out of misguided loyalty will also shun one another.

STRATEGY 3: FOCUSING ON PEOPLE AND PARTS

Understanding other functional areas of your organisation is important to your career success. It will also make you stand out amongst the crowd if you willingly and openly connect with other functions. It might be uncomfortable if you find certain people weird or boring, but it is necessary.

We tend to talk to those we trust and make decisions based on their opinions. But this has a negative impact on culture. Employees need to be encouraged to build relationships across an organisation. Otherwise, it is too easy to slip into a comfort zone of hanging out with people they know.

Introduce like-minded people to each other, proving that you are there to be of service. The objective here is to help everyone in an organisation feel connected and supported to one big community. This is the polar opposite of low trust leaders, who avoid introducing people to each other, as they like to have control over the people they know.

Reflection

- How much do you know about the goals, priorities and challenges of other team leaders in your organisation? What can you do to schedule time in your calendar to better understand them? What else can you do to support your peers in achieving their goals?

- Do you tend to ask advice of people you know in your organisation? Do you have a tendency to hang out with the same people at work? Who else can you reach out to and ask for their opinion?

Implementation

- What areas in your company do your people know little or nothing about? Ask your team members, 'Who would you like an introduction to across the business, to learn more about what they do?'

- In team meetings, ask your team members 'Who else do we need to talk to across the business to brainstorm this idea?'

- Work with your team to encourage working across teams. Ask them, 'What is a small cross-team initiative that we could work on with other teams?'

- Reinforce the importance of learning from others in the organisation by asking your team regularly. 'What have you learned from other teams this week?'

STRATEGY 3: FOCUSING ON PEOPLE AND PARTS

Connect projects

A big issue in large organisations are the sheer number of projects or programs.

An outdated management practice breaks tasks down into component parts, so that individual elements are optimised. What this mean is that employees tend to work on a distinct project segment, with little awareness of who else is working on that project and the end outcome for the client.

When employees 'stick to their own swim lane' it reinforces department separation and keeps people blinkered to opportunities to improve the deliverables to both internal and external customers. Typically, employees will tend to believe that their primary stakeholder is their manager and deliver to their manager.

This creates enormous frustration and bottlenecks for those who understand the broader picture.

This lack of clarity can lead to chronic mistrust and over-commitment throughout an organisation. And I see it everywhere – from medium size organisations that have grown quickly from a start-up right through to large government organisations.

Restructure work so that people work on projects from start to finish. In my work, I've seen again and again that people are much happier in their jobs when they work on a project from beginning to end rather than just one section.

A good question to ask your employees during one-on-ones is, 'What other information do you need to know about the project you are on and who else in the business is contributing to it?'

> *Ensuring visibility around other projects outside your team and the associated roles and responsibilities ensures employees know how to support one another.*

Reflection

- How can you restructure work so people work on projects from start to finish?

Case Study: Putting Connection into Practice

Gary Allen isn't your typical CEO. He didn't go to an elite private school nor get a degree straight after finishing school. He grew up with a dysfunctional father, in a low socioeconomic environment in Melbourne and his family didn't have enough money to pay for school excursions or other school based activities. But the truth was education was not valued by his parents. They thought getting by in life meant getting a job and earning money. There was no belief that either of their three sons were even smart enough to finish Year 12. Not surprisingly, Gary dropped out of tech school at 15 and worked in low paying jobs before joining the army.

One week into his army training, he was put in charge of a section in his platoon. At 17 years old, he discovered that he could excel and take people along with him. He realised he was a quick learner and he would train other trainee soldiers at the end of the day on how to polish their boots and clean their guns. Gary found that people would follow or work with him if he had the right motivation and belief.

STRATEGY 3: FOCUSING ON PEOPLE AND PARTS

Case Study…

After several years in the army, he worked as a truck driver in a mining company. He then ended up managing freight control in an office, moving up the food chain as he outgrew roles that no longer challenged him. Fast forward many years and he was given the opportunity to work at Linfox, a family-owned Australian logistics company.

Back in 2015, on a hot summer's afternoon, I caught up with him to find out how he built trust as a senior leader in this very large company. I asked, 'How do you communicate the vision or strategy to all of your employees?'

He looked at me earnestly and replied, 'How do I do that? I don't know. Three years ago, I built the defence business for Linfox. It was brand new and had never been done before. It was the second time in history it was ever done. I started it as a one man show. I had to deliver a vision, but I didn't know what it was. I had to take one to 1000 employees into the vision to be successful, which I did. I had so many different people engaged in the process – government, suppliers, employees and other stakeholders. A lot of them said, "We did this because of you. Your vision. How you took us through the journey believing that we could do it, when all of us thought we couldn't."'

He continued, "I reflect back on that a lot. What was the secret? I don't have the answer. It must have been in belief. False belief doesn't fly. You need honesty and realism. I said to 20 people at the start, I don't have the answer. I don't know how we're going to do this. But if we do little bits at a time, we will get there."

> **Case Study...**
>
> Gary intuitively used belief mixed in with healthy vulnerability to guide a variety of stakeholders to remarkable success – a technique he has used in various organisations and still uses to this day. He also used connection to link people to a positive future. By harnessing the power of conviction, he lets people know that he trusts them. And in return they trust him in the midst of uncertainty.
>
> What is remarkable about this story is that most people who grow up with parents who don't believe in them tend to not believe in themselves or others as well. Yet, Gary's teenage experience showed him otherwise. It changed his belief in himself and others and propelled him to create a thriving, trusted environment where people work hard in service of a shared goal.

> **Summary: Connection**
>
> At its core, you want employees to deeply understand how the business works. This means explaining how everything fits together, providing employees with both a macro and micro view of their job.
>
> High trust leaders are effectively integrators who deeply understand why the organisation exists (purpose), the required behaviours (values) and the obligations to stakeholders needed to achieve the company vision. They understand the interdependencies and ensure their decisions and behaviours do not negatively impact others.

Summary...

Strategy 1. Linking Personal Impact

It's your job to align each employee's self-interest to a more meaningful and bigger purpose set by the organisation. In other words, you need to ensure they know how their individual talents, values, interactions and effort make a difference. Help people make sense of their lives.

Conversations on meaning – We don't often realise meaningfulness while we are at work. It occurs when we reflect on our work and what gave us joy and what didn't.

In team meetings and one-on-ones regularly ask questions that help people to self-reflect on their job role. Ask:

- What are we/you working on that is personally important?
- What's the point of the work we/you are doing?

Spend time with each of your employees to work out their individual subgoals to achieving the company vision.

Keep people motivated by providing updates on progress made so far, (tell them what they have achieved and not achieved) as well as, how much further to go, (how will we know when we get there?).

If projects are long and have no real milestones, help employees feel that they are making progress through reinforcing what they are learning. If project timeframes are extended, ensure they are aware of benefits or the necessity.

Summary...

Strategy 2. Understanding Beneficiaries

There are both psychological and performance benefits to connecting employees to the beneficiaries of their work. Spending time interacting with beneficiaries heightens worker perceptions of how their contribution impacts others.

Internal Customers – Encourage your direct reports to spend time working alongside internal customers. This will help them better understand how their work makes other people's lives easier or harder.

Some ideas include:

- Have your team members undertake work experience in a different department for a week. Get them to present back to your team what they have learned from their immersive work experience.

- Have your employees do a 'show and tell' of the role of your functional department to other units.

- Have regular meetings with other functional units to share your metrics, how you are each progressing, new ideas and how you need their help.

- Create cross-functional teams to solve problems outside people's normal roles to foster cross-team relationships. This can include working groups and committees that meet regularly to solve issues.

STRATEGY 3: FOCUSING ON PEOPLE AND PARTS

Summary...

External Customers – Ensure your team members spend time talking to customers and learning about what they need from your product or service. Request that employees write a letter to your team as to how they will create customer value through connecting the external customer experience to other internal customers.

You – Strengthening the bonds between yourself and your direct reports is critical to their job satisfaction, as well as your own. You can develop and maintaining healthy working relationships through:

- understanding people better,
- listening,
- assuming positive intent,
- believing in people,
- being vulnerable,
- avoiding affinity,
- watching your reactions.

Strategy 3. Focus on People and Pieces

Help employees understand how all the different people, projects, platforms, priorities all link together.

Explain the purpose – Delineate the purpose in terms of how it makes the world a better place. For creatives talk about how the company's purpose improves customer's lives, enables company donations to worthwhile causes or provides the opportunity to volunteer during work hours. For numbers-driven employees, motivate through connecting the financials to the purpose.

Summary...

Connect teammates to one another – Never assume collaboration will occur on its own. You have to create the right environment. Prime people to work together by telling people that they will be working on a task together, even when technically they might not be really (of course, this is a slight ethical dilemma as it could be construed as lying. Use your own judgement).

Encourage team members to build relationships outside of your team – Help everyone in an organisation feel connected to one big community, through introducing like-minded people to each other.

Connect projects – Reduce people's tendency 'to stick their own lane'. Where possible, restructure work so that people get to work on the whole project from beginning to end rather than just one section. People are much happier when they get to work on a full project.

Key Interaction: Visibility

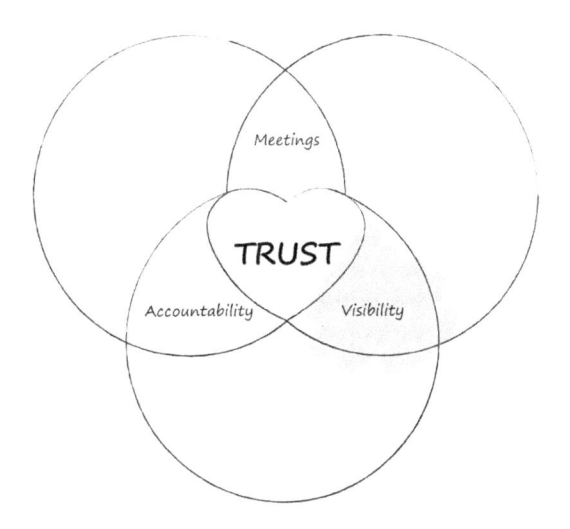

In the *Integrated Trust Building System*, at the intersection between *connection* and *meaningful future*, we have *visibility*. Being a trusted leader boils down to visibility.

Visibility is key to building trust and ensuring *accountability* and *safety*. People believe what they can see. Employees need to observe that they are in a safe place – where there are no secrets, their boss is supportive and people aren't going behind their backs. And that leadership cares about employees.

When employees perceive a lack of transparency, it can really upset them emotionally.

In the work I do within organisations, teams that feel that leadership is visible and approachable tend to be more collaborative. They are also more motivated to solve problems and love their job.

Meetings and one-on-ones are high quality interactions that build trust with those around you but it's also important that you are visible and approachable outside of those dedicated times. And that work is visible as well. This is where visible dashboards become important. Otherwise, you are setting your people and your team up to fail.

Let's unpack what this looks like:

1. Visibility of Information

A major contributor to distrust is when people feel that information has been hidden from them. Ensure that you share as much information as possible (including sources) with your team members. It can be easy to forget to share, making people in your team feel left out. This is particularly the case when you have hybrid teams with some people working in the office and others at home.

> *Make it a general rule to be as transparent as possible, in order to provide the right context for people.*

Share meeting notes, send regular updates and ensure all tasks and expectations are clearly documented. The underlying message is that you are really letting people know that you notice and value them.

2. Visibility around decision-making

Transparency around decisions is critical for any sort of change. Ensure that any leadership decision you make takes your people into account (or provides evidence you went into bat for them). Talk people through how decisions were made. It might seem boring to you, but a lot of employees like to see how decisions were made. Not only does it help them make decisions in alignment with the organisation, but it makes them feel more confident in the leadership direction.

A common complaint is low trust leaders make decisions that don't consider how it will impact employees. Whether you are making a decision as part of a leadership team or deciding on your interactions with direct reports, always ensure you are putting people first and not results.

3. Visibility around priorities and accountabilities

In today's interdependent environment, a lack of information sharing actively prevents teams from talking to each other, assembling a full picture and being responsive. It also contributes to silo thinking and working.

If your team or department serves other internal customers, you can often receive more work than you can handle. When your workload increases, it becomes difficult to deliver work on time and to standard, resulting in other teams not trusting your team to deliver.

For fast-growing organisations, who tend to take on more opportunities than they can handle, visibility and communication around the priority of projects and the progress and clarification of work going forward becomes critical. Otherwise, it can be too easy for mistakes to be made that negatively impact customers. Clear prioritisation helps other teams understand your capacity and reduces tension around resourcing. Be transparent that you will put their work at the back of the queue if additional work appears from the CEO.

Likewise, for a big complex project, it's important that stakeholders know who to speak to about a problem or service. Otherwise, it creates a perception that your team don't want to be accountable or aren't talking to one another.

What employees want is to see evidence that another team is trying to do the right thing by them. This is often an issue in big organisations with an historical culture of only providing information on a 'need-to-know' basis. In a fast-paced environment, teams need to be able to improvise and modify their approach. This can be hampered by a lack of knowledge.

To reduce this situation, provide regular updated information on your team's priorities and deadlines. Have a visible dashboard that shares what projects you are working on. Share the priority order and who is responsible.

The payoff is significant – reducing rework, burnout, stress, bottlenecks, reputation loss, resourcing, unnecessary costs and increasing productivity. It also goes a long way to build trust across portfolios.

Not only that, it will work towards leaders being better at prioritisation themselves. Frequently, I find a lot of leaders have difficulty prioritising what's urgent or important. This can create a lot of issues in fast-moving organisations that take on big workloads.

Visibility of prioritisation and accountability helps employees not only in your team, but also in other teams. It works to provide a common or shared understanding that also provides efficiencies.

4. Be visible

A common complaint that I hear from direct reports about company leaders is that they hide in their office. These leaders sit behind closed doors, refusing to smile or even acknowledge people when they start their day – social niceties that make such an important difference to employees.

Small gestures play an important part in connection. But creating connection is more than just saying hello. It's about creating deeper bonds with each member of your team and helping people feel connected to the work they are doing.

Often, HR professionals tell me their leaders aren't visible because they're introverts. It's a convenient excuse. There is little perceived difference between someone who is shy and someone who is just rude. If you fall into the 'I'm too shy' camp – get over it. Honestly, you're an adult now leading a team, not a primary school kid starting at a new school.

One of the biggest requests I get from employees when I am doing stakeholder interviews is that they want leaders to, 'Just say hello. Ask questions about what people are working on. Be human.' Small interactions make a big difference to employees and must become a weekly structured part of the work leaders do.

Be accessible and approachable. Schedule dedicated times each day when people can call you and get an immediate response. Or let employees know that if they mark their email as a high priority you will respond to it that day.

In a workplace, it is important for leaders to walk the floor and speak to people daily. Employees love to see their leaders and have some form of interaction. Particularly leaders who are running big departments.

Of course, 'walking the floor' isn't always possible if your team is geographically dispersed. But this is no excuse to not be visible. Check in with people each morning – even a quick email or phone call is appreciated by employees.

On that note, all Zoom meetings with colleagues should involve cameras. Having worked with organisations around the world during the pandemic, I have found that organisations that enforced cameras had much more cohesive, high trust cultures. Teams that prefer to keep their camera off will always struggle to build trust remotely.

Furthermore, take up opportunities to be more widely visible within your organisation. Employees like to regularly see both the CEO and senior leaders publicly talking about the vision. Town halls or leadership roadshows are ideal for employees to learn about where the organisation is heading and can ask questions.

This technique is not just applicable to senior executives. It's also relevant for team leaders and managers. Put your hand up for opportunities to speak more broadly to your workforce.

5. Be visible with other leaders

Employees are always watching how other leaders interact with each other. They take their behavioural cues from these interactions, which has a big impact on whether an organisation has separate silos. Ensuring people feel connected to one another also requires showing visible evidence that leadership talk to one another. People are subconsciously checking out leadership behaviours and looking for information that all is well. Reduce the bias people have to assume the worst by championing transparent, visible practices.

What employees want to see is that you are aligned with other leaders and in agreement: around prioritising work, communicating the same vision and working to the same high standards in order to better serve end users. If employees don't see that, they will decide that the leaders don't trust one another. This will impact employees all the way down to the front line. Misplaced loyalty to their boss will mean they tend to not collaborate with other teams because they notice their leader holds back from doing so.

One curious thing that I found when I was working with a large organisation was that employees had a perception that senior leaders didn't like or trust each other. It was based on not seeing much interaction. My advice was that the leaders very loudly pick up the phone and talk to their peers or be seen having corridor conversations. It made a massive difference.

6. Expect visibility from employees

Remote teams are less likely to recover from team members who are not trusting or trustworthy. Of course, if leaders are required to be visible, so are employees. One of the biggest issues with employees working from home is that it is hard for leaders to trust people to work when they can't see them. Not only that, it's also hard for their colleagues to trust them, as well.

In weekly team meetings, encourage each team member to talk about their progress to help everyone understand their contribution to the team. Make each individual responsible for gathering this information and presenting it. This is important because we only trust colleagues who are competent at their job. Encouraging each member to prove their competency will help others trust them.

Take this one step further by encouraging team members to create their own business goals and share them with the team. Ideally, employees have visible dashboards to their whole team that show how they are tracking with their personal subgoals to the overarching vision.

Furthermore, clearly articulate how you expect your direct reports to communicate what they are working on and what they have achieved using the right cadence.

Reflection

- What can you do to improve the visibility of the work being done in your team? What else can you share or make more transparent?
- Employees tend to dislike forced visibility that doesn't seem genuine. What can you do to authentically improve transparency, so that employees feel secure?
- How can you encourage your team members to share their goals or what they are working on?
- What opportunities in your company can you leverage to be more visible? Are there any events you can speak at, any videos you can post or articles that you can contribute to?

Practice 3:
Stepping into a Meaningful Future

How to reduce uncertainty through
highlighting a brighter future

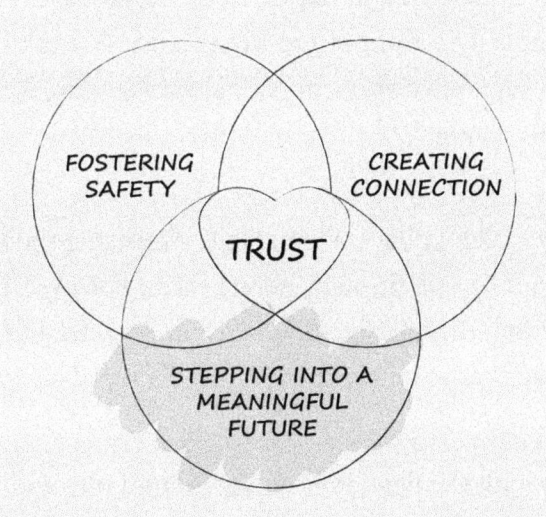

- FOSTERING SAFETY
- CREATING CONNECTION
- TRUST
- STEPPING INTO A MEANINGFUL FUTURE

In a hospital bed lies my father-in-law – an eighty-two-year-old man called Graeme. Shrunken in stature and riddled with Alzheimer's, he is no longer the strong, hard-working dairy farmer who has spent a lifetime doing tough manual labour. He's no longer the man who would fill with tears of pride when he talked about the time in 1987 when he took a $1 million bet on himself and bought 1,000 acres to raise 1,000 cows. A decade later, he would make a further half million-dollar financial investment and build a large automated rotary dairy, reducing his daily toil of milking cows by four hours.

He lies confused, in and out of consciousness from the morphine used to quell his pain from recent hip surgery. A week before, despite being retired for twelve years, he had given his wife, Margaret, a note detailing some strange, but neatly written, instructions to one of his workers.

His will to keep going is formidable, surprising those around him, as he continues to live through poor health. For over 18 months, he has been hurting himself, spending time in hospital and then rallying, only to be back in hospital again, while his mind slowly loses touch with reality.

And now with the pandemic raging around him and Melbourne in a complete lockdown, he is only allowed one relative at a time to visit him late at night. The end seems near, but for so long he has prevailed. Margaret feels this might be the last time, but she's not sure. She stays with him at his bedside and watches while panic spreads across his face. Graeme slowly turns his face to her and lucidly says, 'I can't see my future.' She tells him everything is okay that he doesn't need to know it.

PRACTICE 3: STEPPING INTO A MEANINGFUL FUTURE

Thirty minutes later, when she leaves the room, Graeme finally lets go and passes over.

Trust is about the future and our ability to envision that we have one. As human beings, knowing we have a future provides us with the fuel we need to keep going. If we don't feel that we know what's going to happen, the situation feels unsafe.

In a workplace, feeling that there is some sort of future for us is important for our productivity and wellbeing. To perform at our best, we need to know that we have a meaningful future in our organisation.

Over the years, I've worked with many CEOs across Australia from predominantly midsize companies. Some will complain about their people not being fully productive or trusting others in the organisation. They despair at how their staff gossip and assume the worst-case scenario.

In their minds, these symptoms are frustrating and quite insurmountable (it often gets labelled as, 'Nothing you can do. Just human nature.') But it becomes pretty apparent to me what the issue is and it is often not what they want to hear: people don't know their future at the organisation. And by that I mean on two different levels. The first one is clarity on the big vision for the organisation and where the leader plans to take the organisation. The second is how each person fits into that and what capabilities are required.

That might sound pretty banal. But if the CEO or a senior departmental leader has not clearly communicated the vision that's in their head and how people fit into that, it creates enormous uncertainty and trust issues. The fallout is that people are often unproductive or disengaged because they don't know what they're doing or why it matters.

And it's costly. A lot of people problems in business are due to the failure to show people how they fit into the bigger picture. In the book by Tania Menon and Leigh Thompson, *Stop Spending, Start Managing*, leaders who don't inspire employees with a vision cost an organisation around US$8050 a day.

And it all has to do with our need for certainty.

Craving Certainty

We experience life through receiving information about our environment through specialised receptors and sense organs that pick up taste, smell, visual, hearing and feeling information. All of these stimuli are then transmitted to the brain.

The brain is constantly bombarded with information. To ensure that it doesn't get overloaded it filters out what it deems irrelevant. In familiar situations, neural connections guide our responses to save effort. Most of the time, we operate on automatic pilot.

But there is one problem that occurs when our brains are working in automatic mode. We can miss something important such as a speeding car hurtling towards us.

That's why our brains are designed to be aware of changes. In fact, when our mind stops to attention, it actually releases the feel good hormone dopamine, which gives our brain the energy to switch into, 'Let's work this out' mode.

Our brains are literally like a big computer that's set to work solving problems. While this is a good thing, it becomes negative when the issue we are trying to fix is ambiguous or uncertain. We literally can't relax until we have found a solution. The threat requires extra neural energy to solve.

PRACTICE 3: STEPPING INTO A MEANINGFUL FUTURE

According to a 2014 study, uncertainty disrupts many of the automatic mental processes that govern routine action. The disruption creates conflict in the brain, which can lead to both hyper vigilance and outsized emotional reactivity. People start to worry more – seeing threats everywhere, reacting more strongly to them and conjuring up worst-case scenarios. And if the uncertainty is for an extended period of time it reduces memory, undermines performance and disengages people from the present.

As Jack Nitschke, the study's co-author and an associate professor of psychology at the University of Wisconsin says, 'Uncertainty lays the groundwork for anxiety because anxiety is always future-oriented.'

Human beings crave certainty. Of course, we can never have 100% certainty. The pandemic taught us that any sort of control or certainty that we thought we had was in fact an illusion. Things can change in an instant.

For leaders and managers, it's important to create a *perception of certainty*. Leadership must demonstrate that they have considered the future through discussing their strategic plan together with how they are considering employees future as a workforce. And while you can never guarantee future performance, you can guarantee putting in the right amount of effort and thinking to improve the current situation.

It's vital that you reduce uncertainty by letting people know where the company is headed and why. When employees feel that communication is ambiguous or they don't understand what is expected of them, they fall into fear and low trust.

Employees are quick to complain when communication is unclear, or when they believe they are the last ones to know what's going on or messages are inconsistent. If employees suspect information is being hidden from them, they are more likely to assume the worst-case scenario, which reduces productivity. In fact, a 2016 study by Geckoboard - a visual dashboard company - uncovered that when employees hear nothing, more than half 'resort to doing their own detective work'.

Regularly sharing business plans, leadership thinking behind new initiatives and the proposed organisational structure reduces uncertainty. Transparent communication practices that promote the vision and the steps to get there provide people with confidence that leadership know what they are doing.

People function better when they see strategies and projects broken down into bite-sized steps because they appear less ambiguous. It's like a hiker that needs to reach the summit of a particular mountain. If they are given a map that labels the summit, but does not highlight the paths to get there, it's confusing and ambiguous. The hiker will probably take the wrong turn and get lost. But if they are provided with a map that clearly marks out the mountain and the location of the paths to follow, the task is manageable and the hiker is unlikely to be overwhelmed by their brain's threat responses.

This is why corporate communication must always be focused on reducing uncertainty, particularly when there is a lot of change occurring.

Communicating to Create Certainty

Change is quite frightening to the emotional brain that wants to keep us safe. Leaders who know how to tap in and connect to deep subconscious patterning ensure people trust them and the organisation.

PRACTICE 3: STEPPING INTO A MEANINGFUL FUTURE

> *Typically, when employees resist change it is because management has not comprehensively explained why change is necessary and how it is beneficial.*

The best way to do this is through clear and transparent communication. After all, trust is enabled through communication. But it's not just about telling people about the vision and hoping they get excited. Instead, there are things that the brain loves to hear that move people into the achievement zone of their brain.

Leveraging the Gap

Have you ever watched a bad movie? Even though the wooden acting and clumsy plot lines were frustrating, you still felt compelled to keep watching. You were hooked into finding out what happened next to the hero in the story.

This need to know what happened is called the 'gap theory'. Research by George Lowenstein from Carnegie Mellon University found that humans don't like having an obvious gap in knowledge. Not knowing something is like needing to sneeze, but you just can't. The knowledge gap creates discomfort that we need to fill, as soon as we can.

Curiosity happens when we have a gap in knowledge. So when there is a void between *where we are* and *where we need to go*, our brain is driven to close that gap. It creates tension that drives us to keep searching to find the answer and get closure. It's like doing a jigsaw puzzle. We keep working on putting all the little pieces together so that we can see how they interrelate to create the big picture.

Our brain wants to fill the gap so it can be prepared for any future surprises. Because interest develops from gaps in knowledge, having a gap is uncomfortable. It motivates us to work out how to close it. It sparks our curiosity.

> **And the good news is that leveraging the gap can be used remarkably well to explain change to employees.**

When communicating to employees, the best way to utilise the gap theory is through highlighting two markers on a map – *where you are now* and *where you want to be*.

It's a bit like going into a big shopping centre and searching for a store. You type in the name of the shop into the electronic map billboard. Then, a short movie will play highlighting the journey – or the action you need to take to close the gap.

And that's what you want to do in your communication – introduce the future to people like you're drawing out a 'you are here' map. Take people on the journey explaining what the present reality looks like, what's not working and how things need to work to get to the future.

The best way to do this is to compare the present day, or what's missing in the current reality, to the future. The brain is more easily able to understand complex, abstract information through comparison.

Ideally, you always talk about the future through referencing:

1. *Current state* then *future state*
2. *Gap* then *future state*.
3. *Current state, gap,* then *future state*.

PRACTICE 3: STEPPING INTO A MEANINGFUL FUTURE

These are time continuum beacons that help people focus their attention on an exciting journey to the future that makes their brains feel protected.

Let's drill down into how to do that.

Strategy 1: Understanding the Current State

Envisioning a powerful future that pulls people forward requires being able to see the present unencumbered by delusions.

As Jim Collins said in the book *How the Mighty Fall*, companies that are at risk of failing attribute their success to their own superior qualities ('we deserve success because we are so smart,') – so they stop trying. The downside is if they are wrong, the consequences can be significant. Whereas companies that last a long time attribute their success to being lucky – so they keep working hard. The downside is minimal.

In town hall meetings, CEOs talk about their exciting future plans for the business. But this can be overwhelming for those who are struggling to get on top of their day-to-day tasks. Over-worked employees who are frustrated with using outdated systems and working in an under-staffed team aren't interested in the future, they are too busy surviving. Leaping to the future is not motivating for them when they are drowning because current issues aren't being addressed.

It inadvertently creates distrust between leadership and the frontline when leaders aren't acknowledging current issues. And this is where you come in. Employees often don't believe the CEO or executives, but are more likely to trust what their manager or supervisor says. Your job is to build a bridge to the vision in the way that your team require. A bridge that will be different to other teams in your organisation. Depending on how your team are feeling this could be a little bridge that crosses a pond or it could be a major overpass that spans a chasm.

This is not only for the company vision, but also a new change. You provide the balanced view – both upsides and downsides. It requires customising broad company information so that it is more relevant to your employees' day-to-day work, linking employees with how their work connects to the organisation's mission and what's in it for them. This creates a line of sight enabling employees to understand the big picture.

But more importantly, employees are also more likely to initiate appropriate actions because they understand how their work is directly linked to business results. Employees with a clear line of sight are more likely to provide feedback as the organisation follows a new strategy or initiates major changes.

> **Employees quick response to changing circumstances provides a major advantage over competitors who are shooting in their dark.**

To do this well, there is certain information you need to contrast in the present, in order to motivate people to feel the meaningful future. I want to share with you the four strategies that arose in my research within organisations about the communication employees want.

1. Back the vision
2. Reveal thinking
3. Encourage red flags
4. Observe employees

STRATEGY 1: UNDERSTANDING THE CURRENT STATE

Let's take a closer look at each of these.

Back the vision

In terms of communicating a powerful future for your team, you need to ensure that you believe in the vision.

One of the biggest complaints a CEO has of their team leaders is that they are not delivering the vision in a way people understand. Usually the reason for that is they don't believe in it. And it's pretty easy for a CEO or senior leader to know if this is true because that team leader's team won't be tuned into the whole organisation. Their direct reports give it away when they say, 'Why didn't anyone tell us?' or 'We don't know anything about the vision.'

If you feel that you don't believe in the company vision, then you need to do something about it, because you can't pretend to like a vision when you don't. Your body language and your actions (or lack thereof) will give you away.

In my previous company, I used to direct CEOs and executives when talking to the camera about their latest product or employee safety program. The worst executive I ever had to direct was from a large multinational. He had not learnt his script and was incredibly argumentative and difficult to deal with. One of the things I would look out for when I directed was to ensure that people's body language was in alignment with what they were saying. During a take, his head was nodding 'no', while he talked about the benefits of the new product. I told him about the discrepancy and said, 'It feels like you are not comfortable with promoting this new product. Would that be right?' He then launched into a lengthy tirade of how bad it was and how he hated having to promote something he thought was useless. We ended up having to come back and film him another day, as he was unable to confidently say his piece to camera in the allotted time. Three months later, he was pushed out of the company when the CEO realised he wasn't aligned to the strategy.

There is nothing wrong with not believing a new vision or strategy will work or even questioning it. But it is wrong to make out that you do believe it and that you will disseminate the message to your team and back the strategic rollout.

If you do feel that the vision or strategy isn't right, seek time with your boss or the CEO to ask more questions. A lot of the time it might be that some of the context behind the need for change hasn't been clarified. Ask questions around competitor, business or customer requirements. You want to make sure that you are aware and understand the reasons and the consequences of not changing. Not only for your organisation as a whole, but also for yourself.

During my interviews with stakeholders, a lot of managers will tell me that when they don't understand the vision they just get really nosey and ask people lots of questions. Senior management respect that because it shows that their leaders are keen to do the right thing. Keep asking questions until you feel comfortable with talking about the merits of the direction to your people.

Not only that, observe any sort of resistance within yourself. That can be as subtle as finding excuses not to talk to people about it or as obvious as feeling frustrated (or maybe even angry, like the executive I spoke about previously). Anger is a powerful indicator that something is triggering us.

Sometimes we resist a vision because we don't like change. In his book *ADKAR: A Model for Change*, Jeff Hiatt highlights that the more satisfied we are with the current situation, the more likely we will ignore or discredit reasons for change. While the more discontent we are with the current state, the more likely we will listen to and internalise the reasons for change. Check in with yourself as to where you fit and get support if you are resisting a new direction.

> **The fastest way to move forward as a leader is to accept where you are. Fighting reality is a sure way to waste a lot of time and energy.**

This takes courage because it means owning our fears, our weaknesses and what we can and can't control. It also requires vulnerability as we might have to ask others for help. But being a great leader means making tough choices and being 100% accountable so we are in service of enabling others to do their best work. And sometimes that means addressing our fears, that are trying to keep us safe, but are making it unsafe for others.

And if you find that you just can't back the new vision, then it might be time to find greener pastures elsewhere. Otherwise, you're out of integrity and alignment.

Reveal thinking about change

Once you are confident that you fully back the new strategy, then you need to share your thinking and the thinking of leadership about it.

People love it when a leader has a big, exciting vision for the organisation. It generates enormous energy and pushes everyone forward. But first, employees need to understand the rationale, to ensure it is sound. This provides confidence that the business will survive long-term because leaders know what to do.

As I mentioned before, employees want to know how you and the leadership team make decisions. Not only about day-to-day issues, but more importantly about the future vision for the organisation or a change in direction.

There are a few of reasons for this:

They want to know they can trust your rationale – You hold the keys to their job success. Employees need to know that you are making good decisions for the organisation on their behalf. It also leads to a deeper sense of trust of the company as it shows there are plans to proactively take the company where it needs to go and that no-one is being misled about what these changes require.

They want to think like you – Curious employees want to know your thinking so it can guide them on making the right decisions. Sharing your thinking provides people with a blueprint on decision-making – a powerful training tool.

'The more they know, the more they'll understand' – Sam Walton, the founder of Wal-Mart firmly believed in the power of communicating everything he knew with his employees. Every Saturday morning, he would bring employees together to share as much as he knew about what was going on. He famously wrote, 'The more they know, the more they'll understand. The more they understand, the more they'll care. Once they care, there's no stopping them. If you don't trust your associates to know what's going on, they'll know you really don't consider them partners. Information is power, and the gain you get from empowering your associates more than offsets the risk of informing your competitors.'

As leadership scholar Amy Edmondson says, 'We follow this leader in upheaval because we have confidence, not in their map, but in their compass. We believe they've chosen the right direction, given the current information. And that they will keep updating. Most of all we trust them and we want to help them to find the path forward.'

STRATEGY 1: UNDERSTANDING THE CURRENT STATE

Typically, a manager will tell everyone there is a new vision or change and launch into how it needs to be handled. This can create distrust if people aren't ready.

That's why it's important to start with emotion – why the change is required and the thinking behind the decision. This avoids people falling into sunk cost bias – a thinking trap that causes people to think irrationally. Sunk cost bias occurs when employees can't let go of a project or strategy because they have invested so much time and effort into it. The truth is people are not as interested in information if they don't know why. Knowing the why gets them to lean forward and makes it a much higher priority in their life. You want them to *feel* the need for change.

This is where sharing industry data, assessments, focus groups and stakeholder interviews become important. Externally derived data provides proof to those in denial about the present reality that all is not rosy. It enables people to better understand the changes in the broader competitive landscape and how your products, service and customer interactions need to change.

Alternatively, you could share a story about a frustrated customer who cancelled their order because a competitor offered a less complicated product or more hands-on support. Or you could use an analogy that explains with visuals why the change is required.

It's important to unite the team by providing the meaning behind the work through linking the job to be done to a higher purpose (such as helping customers protect their assets and eliminate financial loss). Through connecting to the company purpose or even the team's purpose, it is easier to hit emotional buttons and get buy in.

Let's look at a hypothetical example of a team leader talking to their team about a change in project direction for insurance software in motorbike dealerships.

> As you know, our goal is to help our customers protect their biggest assets so they don't suffer from unnecessary financial loss (purpose). We thought the software we are working on would be right just for our motorbike customers, (previous thinking). Upon further research, management have realised they made a mistake in their judgement. There appears to be greater demand for the new sales software in both car and light commercial vehicles than previously thought (current thinking). If we were to release the software to motorbike dealerships only, we would disappoint around 55% of dealerships and produce a product that is too short-sighted (proof). There is also feedback from our pilot customers that the product is too complicated to use (proof). We want our customers to be sitting in a dealership and smiling as the dealer shows them how much money they will save on their insurance (future). Our software is not doing that and we now realise that we have to rework the customer interface (current). Longer term, this is the right thing for our customers and our goal to continue protecting their assets. It also means dealerships will be able to better support customer needs. A more integrated software solution is the way to achieve that (future).

Your whole objective is to help people emotionally understand the problem (or opportunity) that is being solved through this change.

> **Trust is a by-product of solving problems.**

STRATEGY 1: UNDERSTANDING THE CURRENT STATE

Employees tend to understand the big picture, but they want more. They want to know about the conversations, options and decisions around how the vision came about. Contrary to most leader's beliefs, employees actually want to know all of the details about the genesis of a vision and what's keeping it alive.

Think of it as being like a contestant on the game show *Who Wants to be a Millionaire*. Contestants go through their thinking process in real time as to which answer option they are considering – A, B, C or D.

While it can be painfully slow, this is what employees want to hear from their leaders – deep dives that show how their leader assesses different options, risks, priorities and how they connect information together.

As a leader, don't hold back from sharing your reasoning about new initiatives and what this means for your team (both good and bad). Share the rationale of the CEO and leadership team as well (if they don't do this regularly). Show visuals of data that backs up thinking. Furthermore, ask for people's ideas and advice on the feasibility of the vision to ensure they feel part of the solution. People love the opportunity to ask questions and share their perspectives.

Encourage red flags

Employees feel more comfortable around a leader who is present, who is truly listening to their issues, rather than jumping to conclusions. It sends the message that you really care about what people are going through and that you are supporting them by clearing the obstacles, so that daily work is easier and more enjoyable.

A lot of leaders find it difficult to stay present. They prefer moving towards the future and bright, shiny things. That's because they are avoiding something – whether that is feelings of not being smart enough or being worthy.

As Christine Comaford says in the book *Smart Tribes*, 'Being present is hard because it can hurt, sometimes we need to deal with things we have been avoiding. The more we address an issue the moment we perceive it, the calmer and more present we are. And the easier for others to follow us.'

If you are living either in the past or future, you won't be focused and will miss opportunities or potential problems. Past thinking is when we ruminate about a discussion that went wrong or fear that things won't work because we tried it before. Future thinking is about what you will eat for lunch or which team members to put onto a new project.

For many visionary leaders, the future can be a place that seems warm and utterly compelling, but we can't get there if we don't take a good look at where we are now.

In my work with leadership teams, I come across plenty of executives who are positive and excited about the vision, generating a palpable energy that excites employees about where they are going and why. They love asking employees about new ideas they have and new ways of doing things. They get excited by a new client being signed up. Yet, there is a flip side to all this positivity. And that is, these leaders don't want to talk about what's not working.

Without even realising it, leaders tend to shut down any negative commentary around a lack of resourcing, system issues or capability gaps. They get a bit cranky with people if they say, 'We don't think we can do it, here's why.' In their minds, those who highlight issues are 'too negative' and best to be avoided.

STRATEGY 1: UNDERSTANDING THE CURRENT STATE

It is much more anxiety-provoking to not talk about issues. It is effectively hiding problems, which can be far more damaging long term. Openly discussing the issues the organisation is facing brings out the best in people. In a great culture, people will want to chip in and solve problems.

Talking about what the company has achieved or is currently doing sets the stage to truly highlight where people are now and where they need to go. It requires talking openly about how people are working together, current capabilities, skills, systems and the impact on customers – honestly flagging issues and problems, as well as what's working. After all, where we lack awareness, we lack growth.

As a team leader, you can often be the victim of positivity in the C-suite. Typically, your team members flag issues with you and you take them up higher to be dealt with – only to have your concern rejected.

> ***Counterintuitively, employees speaking up about issues is actually one of the major benefits of great cultures.***

It is an indicator of high performance because when errors and problems are openly discussed, they can be solved. This ensures the organisation can course correct to avert a potential crisis.

Employees will tend to reject a jump into the future if they don't get to air the company's dirty laundry. They need to be able to air their grievances first before they get onboard the future train. If you are in an organisation or team that is sitting in the abatement zone believing it is doing exceptionally well, it will be hard to have a truthful conversation about what's not working. Be a leader who is willing to talk about issues and not go into combat mode.

Numerous studies tell us is that high performers are often somewhat frustrated with how their teams are performing. They don't fool themselves that everything is going well. It even means being willing to push people to remain dissatisfied with their accomplishments.

And like the old saying 'no pain, no gain', such relentless pursuit of the truth results in a sense of progress, reinvention and growth, which in turn results in a more meaningful and positive work experience. As American entrepreneur and podcaster Tim Ferriss says, 'A person's success in life can be measured by how many uncomfortable conversations she or he are willing to have.'

When we only focus on the good, people become afraid of talking about the bad. This can kill creativity and the will to try new things, which are the mindsets required to lead a high achievement team. Do what you can to enable people to tell you the issues. Those who are customer facing tend to be the first to see the potholes. Yet, our instinct is to avoid telling people bad news. Reward people for being forthcoming and encourage intellectual honesty where possible.

It seems counterintuitive but the only way to enlist people in a brand new future is to connect to the current reality. Warts and all. It's okay to start discussing problems first, particularly if you know you've stuffed up or you've been radio silent. People will respect that more than if you jump into how wonderful things are.

Observe employees

Your direct reports want you to be present and empathetic to the current reality and their experience. But sometimes they are not aware

STRATEGY 1: UNDERSTANDING THE CURRENT STATE

of their behaviours and actions that highlight that they are not fully onboard with a new strategy.

Sometimes we can't take at face value what people say, or even data about employee engagement. We need to combine data with observations and carefully thought-out questions. If you ever feel that data isn't right, because you are seeing or hearing things differently around, then trust your gut. However, spend time really assessing where this thought is coming from – I often see leaders immediately dismiss data because it hurts their ego at some level. When we are coming from ego protection, it shoves us out of reality and into defensiveness, which people will pick up and reject.

> *If there is any employee data, such as low or even high engagement in your team, you want to dig deeper and ask incisive and customised questions for each direct report. Either to know what to improve or keep doing what's working.*

Data is a two-dimensional representation of reality. It will tell you what hours people are working or which teams are declining in engagement. But it won't tell you why. And even if you were to directly ask people, sometimes they can't tell you because they are unaware of their own behaviours or they don't want to be negative. So you also want to observe how your team members are acting.

Empathetic leaders are skilled at reading people or their teams by sensing concerns, moods, dynamics and attitudes. Look out for subtle signs of resistance from employees about the future such as avoiding eye contact with you, not asking questions or just saying that they will work on it (but do nothing). Usually this means there are concerns or fears that you need to address.

This is why having regular one-on-ones is so important. By asking the right questions and having close relationships with your staff, you can pick up issues early and fix them. It's as simple as flagging, 'I noticed you looked uncomfortable about the new strategy when I spoke about it at our team meeting. What was coming up for you?'

Reflection

- Where am I resisting the new vision or strategy? Am I 100% committed to communicating to my direct reports?

- How do I react to concerns or push back around a new strategy? Do I cross my arms or avoid talking to those telling me negative information? Do I get defensive and talk about why the change is good? How can I encourage others to share their concerns without unintentionally shutting them down?

- Do I force the future onto people without giving them space to address present day issues?

STRATEGY 1: UNDERSTANDING THE CURRENT STATE

Implementation

- Share your thinking or that of leadership. Use phrases such as, 'This is our current thinking that is influencing our revised strategy…'

- Provide proof of the need for change (data, customer feedback, industry trends).

- Tell a story or metaphor that resonates with employees to help them feel emotionally the need for change and see themselves participating in the future.

- Invite people to share their concerns and acknowledge current issues, don't refute them. This avoids assumptions and for people to feel the decision has been forced upon them. Allow people to ask questions and weigh in on the decision.

- Observe how people react to change. Don't accept people saying on face value that they agree. Are people taking different action? Are people engaged – asking questions, sharing information and talking about the future goal? Address any issues in one-on-ones.

Strategy 2: Identifying the Gap

The gap is really about honestly assessing what's getting in the way of where you want to go and feeling the discomfort of not being where you really want to be.

We all operate in a comfort zone. What we tolerate in life is what we experience. If you have a team member who always delivers sloppy work or turns up late, it is because you are tolerating those behaviours. The same with if you are upset that people treat you disrespectfully, it's because you are allowing it to happen.

Being a trusted leader means we have to get better at managing poor performance and talking about difficult subjects. It requires having a deep desire to change how we are leading our team and ourselves. We need to spend dedicated time reflecting on our decisions, tolerances, mindsets, behaviours and beliefs. Sugar-coating our current abilities helps no-one – only our ego.

To motivate us, we need to have a gap that creates discomfort. One that is as intense and as challenging as possible. Typically, we only change when we truly realise that what we are doing now isn't working.

To get your team out of their rut, you need to make your team members feel uncomfortable about their situation. After all, if there is no real reason for people to improve, they will quite happily stick with the status quo. To provide people with the energy to get themselves out of their hole you need to help them really feel the next level they need to reach. It's about helping people sense that the current reality is getting in the way of the ideal future. But you need to make it clear what the gap looks like.

The way to do this is to:

1. Ask what's missing.
2. Identify what does success looks like.
3. Discuss the pitfalls of changing.

Let's look into each of these.

Ask what's missing

If you have spoken to people about the new future and then gone into the reasons why things aren't working, it often isn't enough. People will get the theory, but still not take action.

You need to go deeper. And the big one is around what skills, capabilities, interactions or work styles have become outdated and need to be overhauled. While you might have looked externally at the need for change, now it's time to flag where you need employees to pivot. One method I use is to get people to really feel the pain. In my workshops, I encourage people to write down which skills, interactions or communication skills need to improve to get to the future. What's missing? People love to tell you problems and can quite easily write a list of all the areas that need improvement. Then, I ask them to answer the question, 'What are the disadvantages of not changing or improving?' And I get them to list those drawbacks and discuss.

STRATEGY 2: IDENTIFYING THE GAP

But it's not just talking about the problems. Sometimes we can more readily see the gap when we look at what we have achieved and can see how much more there is to go. I like to map this out on a whiteboard to help people see what needs to change.

Again, this is why visual dashboards that show our goals and what we have achieved can be so powerful.

As a leader, we want to create a comfortable working environment. We protect our staff from negative news or avoid questioning those who missed their targets. But employees are smart enough to know that this lacks transparency and accountability. We are choosing comfort over discomfort. And comfort isn't sustainable long term without some painful truths being addressed.

When you have more transparency around how goals are being achieved in the company, employees will want to know why targets are missed. And they expect leaders to own up to missed targets and have the courage to discuss what went wrong and how to fix them.

> **This is powerful because talking about what's not working and your plans to fix the issues publicly is a big motivator to improve things.**

Encourage your employees to also confess when they haven't met their weekly goals and their plans to improve.

Identify what does success looks like

If you have kids or you remember being a kid, you know that it's common for children to pester their parents with, 'Are we there yet?' when travelling to a holiday destination. Employees are no different (except a little bit less demanding). They want to know how much work there is to go.

> **To help them, it's really about contrasting the current reality and what 'good' looks like. This gets people thinking in terms of outcomes rather than activities.**

Workplaces are really a group of people that come together and do activities, but activities (or the doing part of work) aren't as meaningful to employees as the future benefit that will be created.

The best way to is to illustrate what success looks like – before you start work and then after work is completed. It's the pre- and post- of success that helps employees know when they are done – contrasting the present to the future.

For example, say your organisation is improving an app that is currently available for customers. To focus employees on the user experience, talk about the current customer experience and then the customer experience after the change.

For example:

Currently, motorcycle clients sit with the salesperson as they are purchasing their bike. There are lots of forms to fill out. Then, the salesperson uses our software and calculates their insurance premium. They just get told the price. It is not very interactive, individualised or enjoyable. Contrast that to the sales professional who asks some specific questions about their motorbike usage. They plug that data into our app, which then visually displays clear, colourful charts on the computer that show how much money the customer will save by choosing our insurance versus our competitors. The customer can change some of the variables and see a difference in price. Our goal is to create software that sales staff love to use, and which vehicle customers also love because it honestly and visually chooses the right product for their financial situation, ensuring they get the best price.

In some ways, it involves asking yourself the question, 'What does 'good' look like?' and then providing your employees with a clear description of success, so that they are know the parameters and expectations.

This information doesn't have to be detailed, but it vastly increases engagement and encourages employees to think about what that process actually means from the customer perspective. It will ensure that employees make decisions that improve the user experience and have a better sense of their progress and when their work is complete.

You know that employees really get it when they know if their work is done or not. They will tell you that they need more time because they realise something needs more finessing or figuring out.

Again, visual dashboards are helpful tools to demonstrate completed and unfinished work for the team, that motivate employees.

Discuss the pitfalls of changing

People are naturally suspicious of change and innovation, especially when they do not see the long-term benefits.

Talking about the gap means acknowledging the potential obstacles and pitfalls. After all, there is never a smooth and easy journey to a future goal. Honestly discussing the risks and the negative experiences on the road keeps it real. It also makes people more likely not only to expect derailments along the way but also be more open to solving them.

Amy Edmondson says it's about framing work as learning problems rather than execution problems. This requires being clear about uncertainty and how everyone's input matters: 'We've never been here before, we can't know what will happen, we've got to have everybody's voices and heads in the game.'

It links back to what I said previously about believing in your team. Even though you don't know how you are going to reach the goal, you will make it if everyone puts in the effort and works as one.

The reality is achieving difficult goals is hard. There is no such thing as an easy journey to big goals. There will be always be obstacles, unexpected consequences and frustration.

And that's what makes being part of a team so wonderful. We know we have the support of one another to get us through.

Reflection

- How can you make people feel the need for change? What is the most compelling gap – customer needs, industry trends or workforce capabilities?
- Do you believe that your team can achieve the new goal? What do you need to do to increase the belief of you team?

STRATEGY 2: IDENTIFYING THE GAP

> **Implementation**
>
> If your boss has given you a stretch goal that you are not sure how to achieve in the next quarter, brainstorm how to approach it with your team. In your team meeting, share the ambitious target and have your team consider different ways to do it. Ask, 'What are your ideas for reaching this new target? How can we break it down per week?'

Strategy 3: Working Towards a Future State

Leaders often communicate the organisation's future through emphasising ideals and abstract ideas. Words such as 'sustainability', 'innovative', or 'best-in-class' get thrown around a lot – terms that have many different interpretations. The result is that employees tend to ignore them because they provide limited guidance on what to do.

As Chip and Dan Heath mention in the book *Made to Stick*, language is often abstract, but *life* is not. Companies create things – whether that's software, scientific advances or magazines. Even the most abstract business strategy will become tangible actions by employees. And it is those concrete actions that we all understand, rather than some lofty pie-in-the-sky strategy.

Abstraction makes it difficult to understand and remember an idea. The result is that we find it hard to align our activities with others, who may interpret the abstraction differently. Using concrete language avoids these problems.

One way to avoid being abstract is to convey sensory information. Suggestive sensory information helps employees more readily identify with a distant future through evoking sights, sounds, and smells. You want to talk about what the future will look, sound and feel like.

> **Use concrete language such as, 'Imagine our workplace with more smiling employees working at the front desk, wearing our blue uniform and cheering together at the end of a successful and productive day.'**

This helps people imagine the future as something they be a part of. After all, it's hard to imagine the future when it feels distant.

Research by Andrew M Carton, an assistant professor of management at The Wharton School of the University of Pennsylvania found that leaders who communicate growth strategies using image-based words are more likely to succeed with executing the strategy than those using abstract words or numeric goals.

Image-based language paints a vivid picture of the future. It provides the best way to approximate an unknown reality. Employees respond more positively to visions when they are loaded with sensory imagery that highlight the emotional benefits (how it makes me feel) of achieving goals, rather than the functional benefits (what it does for me).

Emotions are fundamental to being a human. People buy based on their emotions. Research has found that rational features only account for 15% of the decisions we make. In the words of Brian Carroll, an experienced marketer, 'People often buy on emotion and backfill with logic.'

Although, most people understand that humans are emotional, what is poorly understood is how to use emotionally based communication on a daily basis to lead others.

STRATEGY 3: WORKING TOWARDS A FUTURE STATE

This is important because when people are thinking about the long-term future, being able to feel it makes it more real. And given the brain doesn't know the difference between what is real and imagined, feeling the future through emotionally resonant words is powerful. After all, as mentioned previously, the part of the brain that processes emotions doesn't grasp language. It only understands feelings.

> *Trusting the future requires being able to feel the positive future it will evoke.*

Using image-based words that include descriptions of people with well-defined attributes (HR managers) and observable actions (smiling as they use their online software) helps people *feel* the vision. In other words, using concepts that employees can literally visualise transports them to the future through stories and metaphors that capture events yet to unfold.

Another study by Andrew M Carton at The Wharton School compared image-laden words ('our toys will make wide-eyed kids laugh and proud parents smile') to wording without visuals ('our toys will be enjoyed by all of our customers') found the image-laden description triggered stronger performance. Image-based words were found to have a galvanising influence – they inspired people to work together toward the same crystal-clear snapshot of the future. While abstract words and numeric goals were not as influential.

Learning how to capture the hearts and minds of your audience is a powerful leadership skill. It is the one thing that distinguishes great leaders from good leaders. People want to be engaged in a meaningful future. As James Woodyatt, the joint managing director of midsize company CDK Stone, mentioned to me, 'Employees want to imagine a new reality and test-drive the emotions that such a future would elicit for them.' And the way to do that is to take them on a journey.

Take people on a journey

Telling narratives takes people on a journey from present to future state. This process translates abstract visions into more conceptual information that helps all employees identify what needs to be done, which in turn encourages action and importantly, care about the outcome. It also stops all those pesky people problems because people know where they're going and what they're doing.

People want the future described in rich detail so that they can select the right path to get there. It's about answering the question in people's heads, 'What will the future look like, feel like and be like when it arrives?'

One of the benefits of communicating clearly to everyone in the company about where you're heading and the challenges and opportunities that the future will bring is that it will better equip people to evaluate how their skills fit into that future. This enables them to consider whether or not that future is one they want to contribute to or if they need to seek new vistas.

There are two ways to articulate the future:

1. Future vision – the overarching goal.
2. Future operating plan – how we will get there.

Future vision – the overarching goal

A clear all-encompassing vision provides your team with the contextual understanding they need to perform in the achievement zone.

STRATEGY 3: WORKING TOWARDS A FUTURE STATE

Essentially, what employees require is a vision that provides a big picture view of where the organisation is heading. It needs to be motivating and not readily achievable. Your CEO will hopefully provide the company vision. Otherwise, you will need to rework it to make it more compelling for your team.

Let's go into an example for a window manufacturing company.

> **A standard vision statement would say:**
> **'To be the most trusted brand for domestic windows across all our chosen segments.' But a more image-based vision statement would say:**
> **'When you drive through streets across new suburbs in metro Australia, you'll see our windows making homes beautiful and light-filled.'**

Notice how the vision is written like it has already happened? When we talk about the vision in the present tense, it is far more compelling. It also helps us get into the prefrontal cortex of our brain that is higher functioning.

Furthermore, you want to include the vision when talking about your company purpose and values. By talking about the end-user benefit, you encourage people to think in terms of outcomes, rather than activities, which is more meaningful.

Future operating plan – how we will get there

The vision also needs to be backed up with important details. Think of the overarching vision as being like a formula one racing car. The car shell looks sleek and fast, but it can't go anywhere on its own. That's where the engine comes in and does all the hard work – planning the work and powering through all the tasks to get to the future. It's the future operating plan and it only looks good to technically minded people. Sometimes the CEO will summarise this, but it is the role of executives and middle managers to work out the finer details.

One of the interesting findings I come across when I do research within organisations is that people want more detail about the future operating plan to support where the organisation is going and why. Employees need this to trust that the strategy is reasonable and achievable.

This can be difficult for visionary CEOs who love to talk about an exciting future (or talk about what the formula one car looks like), but who get bored at putting together detail on how it all works.

Of course, we all communicate and understand information differently. Those on the ground and in middle management positions tend to want more detail about the capabilities required from a career perspective, such as what new hires are needed and what learning and development plans will be put in place. People want to evaluate whether they have the right skills and mindset and if there is a place for them in the future. They also want to know that future backend processes and systems have been designed to support new growth. This is important for employees in high pressure jobs who will resist the vision if they feel that the future is going to rob them of downtime.

As a team leader, it's your role to help each direct report understand how their effort links into the future vision, both broadly and specifically, in terms of their career options. Discuss the future operating plan to support where each individual is going and why, as well as the new behaviours they need to run with, such as more sharing of information or improving quality.

People want to know how they will be affected and how they are expected to contribute. This means confessing if that involves longer

STRATEGY 3: WORKING TOWARDS A FUTURE STATE

hours or throwing away previous work, or if there will be difficult challenges that might first appear unsolvable, which you will work out together as a team.

> *True leadership is about inspiring people with a future where life is easier – a future where there are rewards, provided that people change their behaviours, learn new processes and collaborate differently.*

Talking positively about the future helps people feel as if there is something to look forward to - that all their hard work will amount to something worthwhile. This pulls people in rather than pushing them into distrust. And when you do that, the future is certain.

And what underpins the future? Accountability. We'll delve into that in the final Key Interaction section at the end of this chapter.

Reflection

- How can you imagine the future more vividly? A good technique is to spend some quiet time visualising what the future will look like and what tasks or interactions you will be doing and how that feels.
- What image-based words can you use to describe how your customers will react positively to the new changes?

Implementation

- Test out a new vision in a one-on-one by saying, 'Here's where I see you going as an individual with the new vision. Where do you feel your skills match? Which skills or behaviours you feel you need to strengthen?'

- Another variation is to check for understanding of the vision individually by asking, 'What have you understood from this conversation?'

- Test out a new vision in a team meeting by saying, 'Here's where I see us going as a team. Where do you feel you are going? And where do you think our team should be going? What about the organisation?'

Case Study: Putting Future into Practice

Ian was installed as the new CEO of a start-up that was bought by a private owner. The organisation, which was only two years old, helped business customers get the best price on delivery services. It had grown quickly, starting with the owner and then morphing into 120 people.

The founder abruptly left the business, which caused a lot of angst amongst employees. Previously, he had personally coached employees and modelled a transparent, collaborative culture.

Ian was left on his own to lead 120 employees who still missed the founder. One of his main tasks was to systemise and professionalise the organisation, setting it up for scalable growth, so that it could be sold.

STRATEGY 3: WORKING TOWARDS A FUTURE STATE

> **Case Study...**
>
> A particular area of contention was changing the commission structure for the sales force. This was a pivotal part of the organisation and had not changed since the firm's inception. Ian promised employees he would restructure pays, commissions and contracts to sales and other staff, but the issue was far more complicated than he realised and he stalled. He ignored the big fat documents sitting on his desk that employees supplied to support their case.
>
> Twelve months later, he had done nothing – so employees revolted. The once collaborative culture deteriorated to an 'us versus them' battleground. Employees ignored new directives, took a lot of sick leave and sales dropped precipitously.
>
> That's when Ian brought me in to help him build trust with his people.
>
> The first step was to encourage him to own up to the mess that he had unintentionally created. Talking about the future wasn't working because people were stressed out about current pay. Instead, he need to address the issues with the current state. He called a meeting and let people know that he had stuffed up. Ian apologised and allowed people to frankly share their perspective. He invited their suggestions. It was then that he realised that the task was too overwhelming for him. He had also unintentionally built up so much distrust that he needed someone impartial to mediate. The agreed resolution was to install a new general manager to work with everyone.

> **Case Study...**
>
> Rob was appointed as the new general manager. This more localised approach ensured that solutions were considered from those closer on the ground. Rob acted as the intermediary between the frontline and Ian. He went back and forth, renegotiating contracts with staff, until both sides were happy. It rebuilt trust with staff and the goodwill that had been lost between staff and the previous owner.
>
> Through this process, I helped Ian understand his limitations and how employing someone else with the right people skills and attention to detail had helped better handle past transgressions. He realised that he had unintentionally disrespected employees through not handling their concerns promptly.
>
> Now that we had improved the current situation and Ian had worked on systems to enable growth, it was time to get people into the future. To improve the situation, it was important that Ian increase his communication with staff. This was done through a town hall meeting and regular weekly emails.
>
> The communication touched on:
>
> **Current state**
>
> - Confessing to the errors that he had made and why. This included his emotional response that he was overwhelmed and didn't know what to do (so he ignored the problem). This helped people to see he was human.
>
> - Apologising for the lack of transparency and unintentional disrespect.

STRATEGY 3: WORKING TOWARDS A FUTURE STATE

> **Case Study…**
>
> **Gap**
>
> - Admitting the big drop that had occurred, in both sales and engagement levels, and what he wanted to see them both going back to.
>
> - Highlighting the capability gaps in employee skills that were needed to better serve a larger number of customers to get to the new vision.
>
> **Future**
>
> - Sharing his vision and strategy for the company then inviting employees to share what they thought about his new vision for the business (and what they would improve).
>
> - Letting people know that he believed that together they could create the new vision and create a better workplace environment.
>
> - Explaining with emotionally laden language what the future of working at the company would look and feel like for each employee.
>
> At the end of it, Ian learnt a lot from this experience. He said, 'I have realised the importance of keeping my word on the things that I said I was going to do and just doing them. Even if that means employing someone else to help out because I am overwhelmed and out of my depth. I learnt a costly lesson. I also learnt the power of people knowing my expectations. Sometimes things don't work out the way you expected – funding doesn't come through or the board doesn't agree to a decision. I've now learnt to let people know what's going on, rather than hide it. Trust is a by-product of when expectation and reality are aligned. Distrust is when expectations and reality are broken.'

Summary – Stepping into a Meaningful Future

Trust is about the future and our ability to envision that we have one.

In a workplace, feeling that there is some sort of future for us is important for our productivity and wellbeing.

For leaders and managers, it's important to create a *perception of certainty*. Demonstrate that you have considered the future through discussing the strategic plan and how employees will be contributing to it.

There are three beacons that help people focus their attention on an exciting journey to the future that makes their brains feel safe. Ideally, you always use at least two to compare to the future. This could be current state then future state or gap then future state.

Current state

Explain where people are at now and what's working and not working.

What is the current performance? What is changing – customer preference, competitor environment, government regulations? Why is change required?

Four strategies to effectively talk about the present reality include:

Back the vision – You need to believe in the vision to communicate it effectively.

STRATEGY 3: WORKING TOWARDS A FUTURE STATE

> **Summary...**
>
> **Share your thinking** – Employees want to know how you think through issues and make decisions. This provides confidence in the future.
>
> **Encourage red flags** – Employees will tend to reject a jump into the future if they don't get to air their grievances. Enable employees to share their concerns freely so you can address them.
>
> **Observe employees** – Our non-verbal communication gives away how we are really feeling. Don't just accept what people tell you, ask curious questions when you see conflict between what people say and do.
>
> *The gap*
>
> To motivate us, we need to have a gap that creates discomfort. Typically, we only change when we truly realise that what we are doing now isn't working.
>
> Talk about the gap through:
>
> **Asking what's missing** – Where do employees need to improve their skills, capabilities, interactions and work style?
>
> **Identifying what success looks like** – Contrast the 'before and after' of work to be done for clients.
>
> **Discussing the pitfalls of changing** – Be honest about the work and challenges ahead.

> **Summary…**
>
> *Future state*
>
> Using image-based words to describe the future is more powerful than words without visuals. For example, 'Customers feel proud when they see our chandeliers light up their homes' versus 'Customers like using our lights'.
>
> There are two ways to articulate the future state: future vision and future operating plan.
>
> **Future vision** – Customise the vision set by the CEO into one that is relevant for your team. Use emotionally-laden language to encourage the limbic brain to trust the future. Answer questions: 'Where are we going? What does it look like? What does it feel like? What are the strategic objectives?'
>
> **Future operating plan** – Provide details on what new systems, processes and people are required for the future, so employees can understand how their capabilities will fit into that. Link people's contribution to the future and how the vision will impact them. Let people know what steps the team needs to take to reach the new vision. What does the future operating model look like? What are the future capabilities required? What are the HR processes and back-end systems to support the vision?

Key Interaction: Accountability

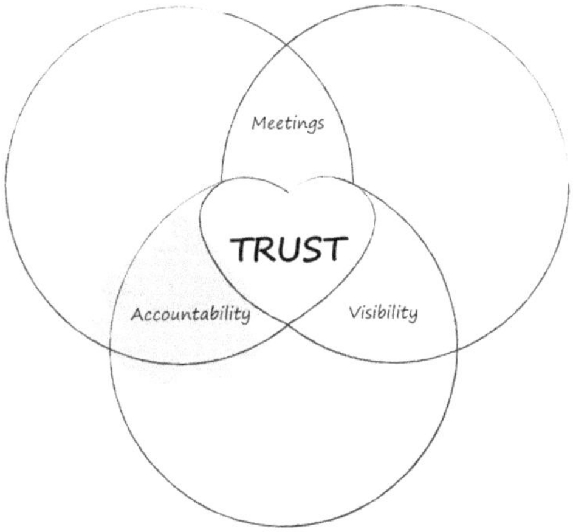

On a grey Melbourne day, six executives and their assistants together sit in a boardroom with four more executives beaming in virtually through Zoom. It is the second workshop that I have run with the team after undertaking some extensive research among employees on what they need from the executive team to trust them.

The 135 people strong company is growing fast, propelled by a close-knit leadership team that works incredibly well together. The company culture they have championed is phenomenal – positive, empowering and challenging.

We are discussing where each executive feels they currently sit in the four team zones – achievement, apathy, abatement and anxiety. To my surprise, two executives confess they are in abatement. They are in a comfort zone that they are finding frustrating. Openly, they admit that it is because they are not being held accountable for results.

One of the main themes that I found interviewing their employees was that accountability was 'fluffy' – there were no consequences or even discussions as to why executives hadn't made their monthly numbers. Employees wanted to know what was being done to rectify the situation, yet messages from the CEO ignored the issue and focused on the positives.

Now, sitting in the boardroom, all eyes were avoiding the CEO, who was visibly squirming in her seat. She is a friendly, energetic leader who loves her company and her people but struggles to find the discipline to keep herself and her people accountable. 'I don't want to micromanage people. I don't want to breathe down your necks and demand you and your team perform in a certain way,' she huffed, almost apologetically, while a red tinge slowly crept up her neck.

As the session continued and we worked through some accountability exercises for the team, she started crossing her arms and pushing her chair away from the table. Then she made excuses as to why she couldn't use the techniques, even though her team were visibly excited at the accountability it would provide for them.

Outside of the workshop, I had a private discussion with the CEO. The good news was that she was aware she was poor at asking for accountability. The bad news was that she didn't want to acknowledge it stemmed from her own dislike of being held accountable. A common complaint that I found in my interviews was that she would never admit to mistakes, and making excuses was her default. True to form, she started providing me with a range of reasons for her accountability dilemma including how she had three coaches to keep her accountable, that she had even being working with a psychologist and it was all starting to be overwhelming.

It was clear that she wasn't ready to be accountable, even though it was the main contributor to the lack of trust within the leadership team and the company as a whole. The curious thing was that her employees all wanted her to rise to the task of making them and their leaders more accountable. They were all cheering her on at the sidelines, but her personal demons were getting in the way.

One of the trademark behaviours of someone with narcissistic personality disorder is that they struggle with accountability. They are unable to honestly own their feelings, apologise, face mistakes and make amends. Blaming others and turning things around is their go-to.

Narcissists are self-loathing with a fragile sense of self. Most of us feel relief at admitting a mistake and doing something to improve the situation. Unfortunately, a narcissist does not have the emotional maturity or self-security to that. Judging, blaming and criticising others is their natural defence. It's a deflective technique that ensures they don't have to look within themselves. But it also stops others from pulling them up on bad behaviour for fear of another confrontation.

According to Brian Tracy, the famed motivational guru, the hallmark of a fully mature human being is to be 100% responsible for their lives. Blaming others and creating excuses for our mistakes is one of the primary causes for failure as adults and a contributor to poor mental health. Instead, by self-examining our behaviour and taking full responsibility for our actions, we boost our mental health and feel in control.

So I'm guessing you're reading this book because you want to create a wonderful, trusting environment with those around you. And I'm also guessing that you have worked with a narcissist and wouldn't want to live that experience again. If that is the case, and you struggle with being accountable, remember that a narcissist can't change. But you can. So being 100% responsible is your goal.

But it's not always easy. We can often be inconsistent in our accountability. Often, where we are accountable provides insights into ourselves – what we like doing and we don't, what we value and what we don't. For example, sales-people who are great at getting on the phone and making calls to warm leads might be lousy at putting in their tax receipts. They value connection, but feel drained at doing admin.

It feels amazing when we make good on our promises and we get things done. Our team trusts us. And importantly, we trust ourselves. But it means doing things we don't want to do. And while you could have a tantrum on the floor when you were six, unfortunately, it is not a good look now.

As adults, only we have control of our lives. No-one else. We might think that we don't have a choice, but we do. We can choose to go to work or not. We can choose to complain about our lot or not. The unhappiest people I know are those who do not accept personal responsibility for their lives and complain about their life. The truth is that when we accept responsibility, we actually feel in control. It increases our personal freedom and happiness.

> **The good news is that if you realise you need to be more accountable then you are on track to improving your results.**

Managing accountability

In the *Integrated Trust Building System*, accountability is at the intersection of *meaningful future* and *safety*. You will also remember that accountability and safety are inextricably linked. Teams that are high in safety and accountability operate in the high achievement zone, while teams that are low in safety and accountability are wallowing in the apathy zone.

Accountability is about providing structure so that people know what is expected of them, in order to deliver to expectations. It helps people feel safe because they know what is required. Accountability also requires visibility of work. Everyone can see the tasks that are needed to be done and who is doing what in service of your big goal. This ensures everyone is getting things done right, propelling you all to a beautiful, sparkly future.

> **Accountability is two-way. It's about demanding accountability and being accountable. You can't have one without the other.**

This means leaders act responsibly and take ownership for results – both good and bad – and employees take full ownership and do their work to the best of their abilities.

You know when there is accountability in your team when people know what it is they are meant to do and have personal agency to get there. They are clear on their job roles, your expectations of the job to be accomplished and how you will support them.

Coaching and a healthy dose of trust, enhances accountability. The more you view your role as helping people grow, the more you will increase their confidence and feelings of personal ownership of their tasks. And when you combine both a sense of individual and collective accountability it helps people feel as if 'we're in this together'.

Leaders being accountable

Leadership accountability is about reducing any sort of hypocrisy that sends a subtle message that there's one rule for leaders and another for employees. When employees feel a whiff of this type of perceived injustice, they automatically distrust the organisation and leaders.

One of the most powerful human drivers is to live in alignment with who we believe we are and who we want to be. When our words and actions don't match, it creates an integrity gap. The bigger the discrepancy the more likely we'll act in ways that go against what we are trying to achieve.

It's common for leaders to overrate how their employees or customers see them. The fallout is that employees will subconsciously distrust their intentions. People need to be able to read their leaders and see consistency in their behaviours, to feel comfortable around them. It much easier to influence others to do the right thing when you do the right thing as well.

It takes a lot of practice and self-awareness to manage the gap between what we say and what we do. It's about managing expectations with present reality.

Leaders must live and breathe the values, purpose and company policies. They can't be an exception to the rule. For example, take a safety manager, who tells people not to be on their mobile phone when walking on the pedestrian zone in the factory, yet regularly undertakes that behaviour. It stinks of unfairness and hypocrisy. It also ensures employees won't follow the rules because leaders don't follow them.

Of course, it's not just company values where leaders must be accountable to results. Leaders must be role models who push themselves out of their own comfort zone, rather than aiming for a 1–2% improvement on their previous goals. They need to pave the way to show employees how work gets done the right way.

Making employees accountable

According to social psychology research by Mihaly Csikszentmihalyi, we need external goals and feedback. When external input is lacking, attention begins to wander and thoughts become chaotic. People who are bored or depressed have failed to develop any attentional habits that might lead to a greater complexity of consciousness.

> *Employees look to their leaders to help with goals, direction and a purpose. They want to be held accountable.*

And yet, one out of every two managers is terrible at accountability. According to study published in *Harvard Business Review*, 46% of leaders around the world are rated 'too little' for 'hold people accountable – when they don't deliver'.

What's interesting is that employees, especially high performing employees, want to be held accountable and receive negative feedback to improve.

So why do we fear making others accountable? One of the main culprits is the fear of being labelled a micromanager. Just like the CEO in the opening story.

It's important to understand the difference between micromanagement and accountability.

Accountability requires people to step forward and provide input. It demands employees fix their work when it's subpar and are responsible for handing in work on time and at the right quality.

On the other hand, micromanaging is when a leader worries about trusting people. They get nervous, disrupting people to check in or taking over, which sends a subtle message that they don't trust them to get work done. Sometimes it's because they have trouble letting go because at some level they want validation for the work they are doing.

Other times it often originates from the desire to do exceptional client work. But it can do a lot of damage to relationships and reduce productivity. That's because it's coming from self-interest and protectionism.

> **The good news is that micromanagement is not a personality or leadership flaw. It is not even a leadership training issue. It's a failure in the basics of delegation. In other words, it's a communication problem.**

Micromanagement is a choice. It's up to the manager to break the habit of micromanagement and control. Reducing micromanagement tendencies requires working on two different areas. The first part is learning how to trust others (or ourselves), while the second is to learn how to delegate more effectively.

Learning to trust others involves empowering people to do their best work and giving them the autonomy to do tasks the way they think best, within some clearly specified constraints. Developing the right mindset is crucial. It requires awareness of your own communication and work style and an understanding of when you micromanage and feel fearful.

A good way to learn how to delegate more appropriately is to use what I call a briefing framework. I started my career as a market research consultant and every project I worked on had a brief that stated the research objectives, methodology, client deliverables and due dates. The brief meant everyone knew exactly what to do, so accountability was never an issue. I have used this framework in all of my subsequent careers and in pretty much everything I need done in my business (including building a home!) It has never failed me.

The benefit of a brief is that it removes uncertainty and ambiguity in a task. When people don't know what's expected of them or get confused, they tend to go off in the wrong direction or freeze. In other words, they get stuck in the limbic part of the brain.

Briefing conversation framework

Essentially, a briefing conversation is an opportunity for open and honest two-way dialogue between the manager and direct report to get to a shared understanding of the project – clearing away any potential derailments or confusion. It's where we talk about our expectations so that those who we have built strong relationships know that there is no wriggle room with an important deadline.

Most importantly, a briefing conversation is an opportunity for you to become an accountability partner for your employees. We are all more accountable when we have someone we want to impress, someone who keeps us on track and checks with us to support our progress.

Being an accountability partner is a wonderful method for any leader or manager to demonstrate to their employees that they care about them. It provides support if they get overwhelmed and want to throw in the towel and also reduces their perception that you are micromanaging.

When providing directives about projects, you want to follow an accountability structure.

1. Start with writing the brief (on your own) – Depending on the complexity of the project, you want to get yourself clear on expectations, objectives, constraints, milestones, what success looks like, how they should achieve the task and how you'll measure success. I like to write down everything that is required, to ensure that it is clear in my head, from small tasks right up to large. Also, connect it to the vision and purpose so they can make decisions from the big picture perspective (outcome) rather than just getting a task done.

2. Discuss the brief – This is the most important part. The goal here is to ensure you both have the same shared understanding and that they are very clear on your expectations. Schedule in time to go through the document. It should be an engaging conversation where your direct report gets to ask questions and you can check in with them to ensure they are on the same wavelength. Ensure you provide some autonomy by letting them decide on how a task can be done. It's also where you clearly define what success looks like, so there is no confusion around expectations. Say, for example, your subordinate is working on a client report. Define the client world now (including strengths of the situations, issues and limitations) and compare it to what their world will be like afterwards. You can also define what personal success looks like for them, in terms of how you'll reward them, such as more work, promotion or more client-facing opportunities.

3. Reduce risks – Make sure that you are not setting people up to fail (or yourself). Check in with them to make sure that they have the right level of capability and confidence. Often, delegation goes awry when managers and employees are both overly hopeful. If the work is new to them, ask them how confident they feel about whether they have the right skills or resources. Ask them what they feel might be missing and then create a plan with them to fix any gaps. If the gaps are too big or the goal is unrealistic, delegate to someone else. Better to do that now, then regret it later. If this is your first time working with them, make sure you are not putting them on a high stakes project. Start with low risk.

3. Create milestones to track results – Accountability is heightened when it is visible. The best way to ensure there is accountability is to put together a calendar with milestones. This can be an online dashboard or even a worksheet. Work out together what the measurements for success are and deadlines. Say for example you have worked out your team member's three main goals for the quarter, you want to have some sort of form for them to fill out so they can see they are making progress. It could be a form where they fill out the number of people they have contacted or the number of proposals they have created. Work together to decide on how progress can best be communicated to you.

4. Bake in progressive feedback – Sometimes direct reports can be afraid to ask for help or an unseen issue pops up. During the briefing conversation, schedule regular check in points to ensure that they are on track. This will also stop you from checking in with them unannounced and creating chaos. As leadership coach Marshall Goldsmith says, 'Follow up is how we change. It's how you measure progress and remind people that we're making an effort to change and that you're there to help them.' With clear measurements and expectations in place, it should be easy to see if they are delivering on their commitments. If any of their targets slip, you have time to fix it immediately with their input. Feedback is two-way and provides a perfect opportunity for you to offer more support and advice. Asking, 'What can I do to help?' or 'Is there anything you are stuck on?' goes a long way to ensuring they know you are there for them.

5. Articulate clear consequences – This is what a lot of leaders forget to make clear as they assume consequences are implied. Without consequences, people are more likely to make excuses and rationalise why they couldn't make the deadline. There needs to be clarity around what happens if they fail to deliver the goods on time or at the right level of quality. Ideally, it's also tied into how it will personally impact them. It might be that if they fail to get the work done well, it can impact your customer's ability to launch a new product on time. The impact being that they personally will not be able to get stretch assignments. Other consequences might be that they don't get to attend an important client meeting or training workshop. Of course, if they do well at the task, you can let them know that it will provide them with great careers skills, you will reward them with more important work or opportunities to understand the business and customers better. Whatever it is, make sure they are aware of the meaning and importance of the work involved – both to customers and themselves. Public recognition and celebration is also powerful.

The goal with accountability to ensure everybody knows what is expected of them, so they lead themselves. If they see an issue, they fix it. Employees understand what high quality work looks like and work towards it.

When accountability is clear, it provides employees with the structure and security they need to perform at a higher level. It even makes them feel trusted which works towards them doing their best for the team and being loyal.

Reflection

- Where am I good at accountability? Where do I drop the ball? Are there certain times when I avoid accountability? For example, late in the day, when it's demanded rudely.

- What excuses do I make when I'm avoiding being accountable? Are they the same each time or different? What's the same?

- How would being more accountable improve my life? What about the lives of my family? Or team members?

- When do I tend to fear handing control over to others? For example, is it for work I take pride in completing? Is it when I feel guilty for not doing it myself? Is it when I'm fearful poor work will be a bad reflection on me?

Implementation

One-on-ones

- Discuss what success (including quality) looks like for the team and how their tasks connect to that.

- Explain their role and responsibilities, and your expectations. Encourage them to repeat back to you what they believe them to be, so you can check for accuracy and understanding.

- Clearly articulate how employees need to communicate progress with you. For example, do they need to send you a summary email of work done at the end of the week or would you prefer a daily phone call?

Wrapping Up and Next Steps

Humans are social creatures who love to communicate with each other and hang out. Our happiest memories are when we work with others in the pursuit of an impossible dream.

But fear and self-loathing lock us into our own little boxes, making us feel disconnected and alone. We behave badly towards others – acting jealous, entitled or just bad-tempered. We feel unworthy or incapable of achieving our goals. And if we let it, that uncomfortable space becomes our comfortable reality.

And that's where *you* make a difference – through your energy and focus to create a healthy, high trust team culture. A great team leader helps those around them make sense of their lives through goals, purpose and action. They foster a thriving, connected, accepting workplace that gently coaxes people out of their protective shells to gleefully join in with others, leaving their fears and self-doubt behind.

As human beings, we all want to be trusted. Our deepest need is to be visible, to feel heard and that we belong. We want people to trust us to do a good job, to value what we do and involve us in their future plans. We want to feel that we can shape our future and of those around us – that we have control over our destiny.

Transitioning your team to the high achievement zone means rethinking and reworking the interactions with and between your employees. Relationships are a social contract. All parties are responsible for the effectiveness and energy of a team. You take the higher ground, demonstrating and demanding accountability with how people need to behave and deliver work, while employees do the best work they can and play nicely with others. This requires breaking through people's individualistic, protective tendencies that can go against team performance.

Moving to the achievement zone means changing how you lead your team and how they work together. It means creating an environment where there are multiple signals that people are safe, connected and have a bright future together. It talks to people's hearts - soothing them with the important non-verbal message 'we're stronger together.'

When you do that you don't have to fix individual behaviours so much, people will gravitate to what the collective is doing. After all, change occurs more easily in supportive groups. We don't change on our own.

This requires making it clear to team members that:

- It's not about *what* we communicate, it's *how* we communicate with one another.
- It's not about *who* is on the team, but *how* we interact.
- It's not about *smart individuals*, but about us *working smarter together*.
- It's not about *learning once*, but how we keep *improving and learning from one another*.
- It's not about *what you know*, but how much you can leverage and access *what other people know*.

As a leader, your job is to create an environment where people work together in service of a shared goal – a high achievement environment where people wake up in the morning excited about going to work and hanging out with others equally excited by the opportunity to learn, experiment and solve complex problems.

We live in a diverse and complex world. Everyone is different. Some people might require more trust building than others, while others need less. The good news is that you don't have to navigate the complex psychology of humans – or even yourself. Ultimately, you cultivate trust by how you make people feel. We process whether we can trust someone through our emotions. We don't trust others by what they say, it's how they make us *feel*. Their consistent actions that show they care about our wellbeing determine whether we feel we can or cannot trust them.

> **Remember, you can't talk your way into trust; you have to behave your way into it.**

Today, leaders need to reassure people that their emotional needs are being met through both verbal and nonverbal communication. Essentially, they communicate that the organisations cares about people, not profit, that they care about their direct reports – their career pathway, mental health and job satisfaction. This involves leaders communicating to the part of the brain that manages trust, the limbic brain, which is part of the brain that doesn't understand language, but feelings.

And it requires that you focus on creating safety, connection and a meaningful future. Asking yourself weekly:

- *What do I need to do to create safety for my team? How do I foster safety for each individual? What do I need to feel safe?*

- *How can I ensure people feel connected to one another? And how can I better connect the work to be done within our company? How can I ensure I stay connected to people?*
- *How can I communicate the future for each individual in my team? What's the best way to help my team feel excited about our future? How can I feel that I have a future at this organisation?*

You emotionally signal to your people that 'we're all in this together' through asking questions each week, in meetings and one-on-ones, and through improving visibility of work, being approachable and demanding reciprocal accountability.

And it is not through telling people that they are valued, safe and connected.

It also has to be backed up with consistent action. Otherwise, people will distrust you and disengage.

The key is to start with small steps that you keep building upon. Try new things slowly and experiment. Understand that there is no finish line – trust is a process, not a single event – and that these behaviours need to become part of who you are, not what you do when others are watching.

It also means observing employees and how they behave with one another. And it requires self-reflection on what you're doing well and what needs improvement.

It has been my intent to help improve your self-awareness and conversations with your team members and peers. Now it is up to you to do the work through practising one new question each week. There are plenty of free resources to download from my website to help keep you on track.

And when you truly embody these behaviours, you will know. Because when you step back and observe your team you will see the magic unfold. People will be working harmoniously together, energised by the need to solve problems to their highest abilities and serve the client at the highest level. You will have a team that feels trusted to thrive. Lead by you: a trusted and connected leader.

Further Resources

I have put together some helpful resources. Go to www.marie-claireross.com/ttt-book-resources. You will find a variety of articles, assessments, checklists and self-reflections tools. Here's a sample:

- Worksheet for bringing together current, gap and future
- The anatomy of a great one-on-one (article)
- Accountability brief
- Trusted leader self-assessment
- Weekly self-reflection tool.

Weekly leadership tips

If you enjoyed this book, then you might be interested in my other writing. I post weekly leadership articles on my blog. If you subscribe, you will be the first to hear about new research, ideas and my newest books. You can sign up at: marie-claireross.com/blog-subscribe.

Connect with Me

Congratulations on finishing this book. I always feel so humbled by people who read my work. It means that you want to be a better people leader or inspire others to be better leaders.

And the more people who are on the planet practising these techniques, the better this planet will be! I reckon we will get to world peace – but you can challenge me on that one.

When I am not writing, I am working with leaders and organisations to implement the concepts in this book through a variety of programs. If you feel that one of my speaking, training or coaching programs could help your team, get in touch through my website and let's have a chat!

www.marie-claireross.com

.

You can also connect with me on LinkedIn.

To you and your team's success!

XX

Marie-Claire

Also available from Marie-Claire Ross

Transform Your Safety Communication is for safety leaders and communicators who are frustrated with inconsistent and uninspiring safety messages that get ignored. This book provides safety professionals with the necessary skills to get people to listen, understand and remember their safety messages, in order to change safety behaviours. This no-nonsense guide is packed with tips and easy-to-use templates. Find out the key requirements of safety communication and learn how to instantly apply the techniques by using the done-for-you templates.

Available in print and eBook formats at: https://www.marie-claireross.com/transform_your_safety_communication

Book List

Here is a list of the books I've mentioned throughout this book that are worthwhile reading.

ADKAR: A Model for Change in Business, Government and our Community, Jeff Hiatt

Flow, Mihaly Csikszentmihalyi

Good Authority: How to Become the Leader your Team is Waiting for, Jonathan Raymond

High Output Management, Andrew S Grove

How the Mighty Fall: And Why Some Companies Never Give in, Jim Collins

Insight: The Power of Self-Awareness in a Self-Deluded World, Dr Tasha Eurich

Made to Stick: Why Some Ideas Survive and Others Die, Chip and Dan Heath

Powerful: Building a Culture of Freedom and Responsibility, Patty McCord

Smart Tribes: How Teams Become Brilliant Together, Christine Comaford

The Culture Code: The Secrets of Highly Successful Groups, Daniel Coyle

The Fearless Organization: Creating Psychological Safety in the Workplace for Learning, Innovation, and Growth, Amy Edmondson

The Leadership Challenge: How to Make Extraordinary Things Happen in Organizations, James M Kouzes and Barry Posner

The Power of Bad: How the Negativity Effect Rules Us and How We Can Rule It, Roy F Baumeister and John Tierney

The Power of Habit: Why we Do What we Do in Life and Business, Charles Duhigg

The Right (and Wrong) Stuff: How Brilliant Careers are Made and Unmade, Carter Cast

Understanding and Building Confidence, Charlie Wardle